Cooking Italian

PASTA

THUNDER BAY
P·R·E·S·S

Editorial Director: Cristina Cappa Legora
Editorial Coordinator: Valeria Camaschella
Translation: Studio Traduzioni Vecchia, Milan
North American Edition
Managing Editor: JoAnn Padgett
Associate Editor: Elizabeth McNulty

Table of Contents

First published in the United States by

Thunder Bay Press
5880 Oberlin Drive, Suite 400
San Diego, CA 92121-4794
1-800-284-3580
http://www.advmkt.com

ISBN 1-57145-195-1

Library of Congress Cataloging-in-Publication Data available upon
request.

Printed in Singapore

1 2 3 4 5 99 00 01 02 03

Introduction

Cooking is a necessity and a pleasure. Or rather, necessity is transformed into pleasure. Today, we like to try out new ingredients whenever we can, inventing variations on traditional dishes, and experimenting with unusual types of cooking procedures.

This new series of books was designed to make cooking a pleasant pastime, with recipes based on our tradition that nevertheless often contain a little something extra, a flash of imagination, an exotic variation that makes the dish more appetizing and impressive.

The books you'll peruse will include a number of tools to help you achieve the best possible results without making mistakes or wasting time. First of all, look at the summary in each section, which will give you an immediate overview of the dishes included. The color illustrations will help you quickly choose the recipe you like best.

The recipes themselves are designed to be as practical as possible. The ingredients are clearly listed to the side, followed by the equipment necessary and a practical chart that summarizes everything you need to know right away, before you begin cooking: the degree of difficulty, preparation and cooking time, cooking method, how long the dish will keep, and so on. The description of the recipes is also extremely clear and detailed, and is divided into sections that cover each separate stage of the recipe.

Another important feature is the suggestion of an appropriate wine to be served with the dish. (These are just suggestions because we all know that wines are a matter of personal taste.) To make it easier for you, we have always selected wines with appellation contrôlée, with the official caption. Of course, we also provide the best temperature for serving each individual wine.

In addition, there are always practical, useful suggestions on the recipe itself (for example, whether you can change any ingredients, how to multiply a given dish), or related to preparation (for example, how to prevent ravioli from breaking as they cook).

Finally, we include a "special note" for each preparation—some extra information on an ingredient in the recipe that may be historical, scientific, dietetic and so forth—that further enriches the descriptions.

This book is devoted to PASTA, the queen of our tables. Divided into Long Pasta, Short Pasta, and Baked and Stuffed Pasta, we offer you a festival of dishes that will truly allow you to enjoy yourself in the kitchen, as you surprise your friends and family.

Recipe Index

With Asparagus and Almonds p32

With Zucchini p33

With Potatoes and Kale p34

With Red Pesto p36

With Almonds p38

With Basil p40

Pie p42

With Roses p44

With Walnuts and Gorgonzola p45

Long Pasta

Green Taglierini
(Fine Noodles) in Fondue

INGREDIENTS
serves 4

Sauce
10 1/2 oz. FONTINA CHEESE
1 cup — 0.25 l MILK
3 EGG YOLKS
1 WHITE TRUFFLE, sliced thinly
SALT and PEPPER to taste

For the pasta
3/4 lb. — 300 g SPINACH
2 cups — 220 g WHITE FLOUR
2 EGGS
pinch of SALT

EQUIPMENT
tall, narrow container
saucepan, casserole dish
double boiler
pot, serving dish

Difficulty	**AVERAGE**
Preparation Time	**50 MIN. + 1 1/2 HOUR**
Cooking Time	**20 MIN.**
Method of cooking	**STOVETOP**
Microwave	**NO**
Freezing	**NO**
Keeping Time	**1 DAY**

SPECIAL NOTE
Fondue is a traditional dish in the cuisine of the Valle d'Aosta region. There are variations in other regions as well, such as Vallese in Switzerland, where kirsch is added to the ingredients.

RECOMMENDED WINES
Valle d'Aosta rosato: rosé served at 57°F / 14°C
Trentino Cabernet Franc: light red wine served at 61°F / 16°C

1 Cut the fontina into thin slices, place it in a tall, narrow container, cover it with the milk and let it stand for an hour. Clean the truffle by scrubbing it, washing it well and drying it. Chop the spinach, wash it and cook it for 3 minutes. Squeeze it and mince. Then place it back in the saucepan and dry it over moderate heat, stirring often. Sift 1 3/4 cups / 200 g flour on the rolling board, and place the egg, the salt and the spinach in the center. Work the ingredients until you have an elastic, homogenous dough. Wrap in a cloth and let it rest in a cool place for 30 minutes. Take it out and roll it to a thickness of about 1/8 inch / 2–3 mm. Flour the surface of the sheet of dough, roll it up and, using a very sharp knife, cut out taglierini about 3/4 inch / 1 cm wide.

2 Drain the fontina and place it in a double boiler on the burner, with 3 tablespoons of the milk until covered and the egg yolks, then mix. The fontina will melt, forming threads, then will become almost liquid, and then will become thick. When the fondue becomes creamy, remove from the flame, add a pinch of white pepper, and mix. Bring a generous quantity of salted water to boil in a pot, add the taglierini and cook until done. Drain and place on the serving dish. Cover with the fontina sauce and sprinkle with the thinly sliced white truffle. Serve hot.

PRACTICAL SUGGESTIONS
For the fondue to be successful, it should not thread, but should have a creamy texture. Generally it is not salted, but try it first, and if necessary add a pinch of salt.

Mushroom Linguine with Walnuts

RECOMMENDED WINES

Colli Berici Tocai (Veneto): dry white wine served at 61°F / 16°C
San Severo rosato (Puglia): rosé served at 57°F / 14°C

1 Trim, wash and chop the onion. Sauté it in a frying pan with a tablespoon of the oil, the peeled, crushed clove of garlic and spices. Cook until the onion begins to brown.

2 Clean the mushrooms, wash them quickly, dry them and chop into small cubes. Add them to the onions and garlic and cook for 10 minutes, mixing occasionally with a wooden spoon. Add the peeled, chopped tomatoes, a pinch of salt and freshly ground pepper and cook 10 more minutes.

3 In the meantime, heat the remaining olive oil in a small saucepan and sauté the coarsely chopped walnuts for 4–5 minutes, until they begin to grow golden. Remove from the flame and add to the sauce.

4 Bring a large amount of salted water to boil in a pot, add the linguine and cook al dente. Drain, place into the serving dish, add the sauce and mix, mixing the pasta and sauce well. Sprinkle with the rest of the walnuts and the finely minced parsley and serve immediately.

PRACTICAL SUGGESTIONS

In the quantities indicated, this is an excellent single dish that you can follow with a big plate of steamed vegetables seasoned with a bit of extra virgin olive oil.

INGREDIENTS

serves 4

1 large ONION
3 tablespoons EXTRA VIRGIN OLIVE OIL
1 clove GARLIC, crushed
minced PARSLEY
1 teaspoon CINNAMON
1 teaspoon ALLSPICE
1 teaspoon fresh grated GINGER ROOT
3/4 lb. – 250 g MUSHROOMS
16 oz. – 450 g TOMATOES (canned peeled
tomatoes can be used)
SALT and PEPPER to taste
1 1/2 oz. – 40 g WALNUTS
1 1/2 lb. – 500 g LINGUINE

EQUIPMENT

frying pan, saucepan
pot
serving dish

Difficulty	AVERAGE
Preparation Time	30 MIN.
Cooking Time	40 MIN.
Method of cooking	STOVETOP
Microwave	NO
Freezing	NO
Keeping Time	2 DAYS

SPECIAL NOTE

Allspice is the fruit of *Pimenta officinalis*, which is gathered before it ripens and sun–dried, then used to season spicy sauces. It is also known as Jamaica pepper.

Spaghetti Salad

INGREDIENTS

serves 4

1 lb. – 400 g SPAGHETTI
1 tablespoons EXTRA VIRGIN OLIVE OIL
3 1/2 oz. – 100 g GREEN and BLACK OLIVES
1 6 oz. CAN TUNA IN OIL
1 oz. – 50 g CAPERS IN SALT
SALT and PEPPER to taste
1 HOT PEPPER

EQUIPMENT

pot
bowl
chopping knife
serving dish

Difficulty	EASY
Preparation Time	15 MIN.
Cooking Time	10 MIN.
Method of cooking	STOVETOP
Microwave	NO
Freezing	NO
Keeping Time	2 DAYS

SPECIAL NOTE

Hot peppers contain the alkaloid capsaicin, which gives it the spicy flavor that sometimes is too much for our palates to tolerate.

RECOMMENDED WINES

Trebbiano di Romagna (Emilia): dry white wine served at 50°F / 10°C
Etna bianco (Sicily): dry white wine served at 50°F / 10°C

❖

1 Bring a large quantity of salted water to boil in a pot, add the spaghetti and cook al dente. Drain, place back into the pot and season with a bit of olive oil, mixing well with a large fork to prevent it from sticking.

2 In the meantime, drain the tuna, place in a bowl and crumble coarsely with a fork. Remove the olive pits and the salt from the capers, then chop them.

3 Add these ingredients to the spaghetti, add the pepper and minced hot pepper and mix thoroughly. Place in a serving dish and serve. If you want to eat the pasta salad cold, cool for several hours.

PRACTICAL SUGGESTIONS

To prepare this pasta salad, you can also use other ingredients to your taste, perhaps julienne vegetables (sliced into very thin strips) and pickled vegetables. If you want a more delicate flavor, use tuna packed in spring water rather than oil.

Thin Spaghetti Salad with Arugula

INGREDIENTS
serves 4

Vinaigrette
SALT and PEPPER to taste
2 tablespoons APPLE CIDER vinegar
6 tablespoons EXTRA VIRGIN OLIVE OIL
1 clove GARLIC

8 MEDIUM TOMATOES
1 RED ONION
1/2 lb. – 200 g ARUGULA
1 lb. – 350 g THIN SPAGHETTI

EQUIPMENT
bowl
2 pots
mixing bowl
serving dish

Difficulty	AVERAGE
Preparation Time	15 MIN.
Cooking Time	10 MIN.
Method of cooking	STOVETOP
Microwave	NO
Freezing	NO
Keeping Time	1 DAY

SPECIAL NOTE
Perhaps of remote Chinese origins, spaghetti became common in Sicily in the 17th–18th centuries, and then spread throughout southern Italy (especially Naples), and gradually to the North as well.

RECOMMENDED WINES
Orvieto classico (Umbria): mellow, aromatic white wine served at 54°F / 12°C
Solopaca rosso (Campania): light red wine served at 57°F / 16°C

1 Prepare the vinaigrette. Place the salt, apple cider vinegar and pepper in a bowl, and mix until the salt is completely dissolved. Add the olive oil, the peeled, sliced garlic and lightly beat with a fork until the dressing is emulsified and homogenous.

2 In a pot with boiling water, scald the tomatoes for a few minutes, then drain, remove the skins, seeds and liquid and cut into chunks. Peel the onion, wash, dry and chop. Wash the rocket and cut into strips with a very sharp knife.

3 Cook the spaghetti in a pot with a large amount of boiling salted water. Drain when it is cooked al dente and place into a mixing bowl. Add the chopped tomatoes, the onion and the rocket. Season with the vinaigrette, mixing quickly to blend the ingredients, then transfer to a serving dish and serve.

PRACTICAL SUGGESTIONS
If you want to add an exotic note to the vinaigrette, add a teaspoon of freshly grated ginger root.

Spaghetti with Olive Paste

INGREDIENTS

serves 4

1 lb. – 350 g SPAGHETTI
6 tablespoons TOMATO PUREE
1 clove GARLIC
1 tablespoon OLIVE PASTE
1 tablespoon minced PARSLEY
2 tablespoons EXTRA VIRGIN OLIVE OIL
GRATED PARMESAN CHEESE to taste
SALT to taste

EQUIPMENT

pot
frying pan
serving dish

Difficulty	EASY
Preparation Time	5 MIN.
Cooking Time	20 MIN.
Method of cooking	STOVETOP
Microwave	NO
Freezing	NO
Keeping Time	2 DAYS

SPECIAL NOTE

Olives are an oval–shaped drupe from 1.5 to 3 centimeters long, with a green skin before maturity that later becomes purple, brown and smooth.

RECOMMENDED WINES
Riviera Ligure di Ponente Vermentino: dry white wine served at 50°F / 10°C
Biferno bianco (Molise): dry white wine served at 50°F / 10°C

1 Bring a large amount of salted water to boil in a pot, add the spaghetti and cook al dente.

2 In the meantime, prepare the sauce. Cook the tomato puree and the peeled clove of garlic for 10 minutes, add 2 tablespoons of the pasta cooking water, the olive paste and the minced parsley, and mix well with a wooden spoon to blend the ingredients. Add the oil and remove from the heat.

3 Place the well–drained spaghetti directly in the pan with the sauce and brown for one minute, seasoning it well. Transfer it to the serving dish and serve, garnishing with sprigs of fresh parsley and sprinkling generously with grated parmesan cheese.

PRACTICAL SUGGESTIONS
You can substitute the olive paste with 4 oz. / 100 g pitted, minced black olives, or with a level tablespoon of tahini (sesame butter), which will give the dish a Middle Eastern flavor.

Bavette with Bacon and Mushrooms

INGREDIENTS

serves 4

3/4 lb. — 300 g MUSHROOMS
2 oz. — 50 g CHUNK OF BACON
1 tablespoon minced PARSLEY
1/8 cup — 20 g BUTTER
SALT to taste
1 lb. — 400 g BAVETTE
(pasta in the form of thin strips)
2 EGG YOLKS
pinch of RED PEPPER
2 tablespoons GRATED PARMESAN CHEESE

EQUIPMENT

pot
cast iron skillet
large frying pan

Difficulty	AVERAGE
Preparation Time	10 MIN.
Cooking Time	20 MIN.
Method of cooking	STOVETOP
Microwave	NO
Freezing	NO
Keeping Time	1 DAY

SPECIAL NOTE

Mushrooms have been cultivated since ancient times. The Greeks and Romans grew the species Pholiota aegerita (the piopparello, or "poplar mushroom") by pouring warm water and wine on poplar wood.

RECOMMENDED WINES
Chianti classico (Tuscany): medium–bodied red wine served at 64°F / 18°C
Dolcetto d'Asti (Piedmont): light red wine served at 61°F / 18°C

❖

1 Remove the earthy part of the mushrooms, wash them, dry them gently with a dish cloth and slice. Trim the parsley. Wash and mince.

2 Chop the bacon into small cubes and cook over a rather high flame in a cast iron skillet until they are crispy, then drain all but one tablespoon of cooking fat and remove the bacon from skillet. Add the mushrooms to the skillet and cook for 2–3 minutes over a high flame, stirring them occasionally with a wooden spoon. Finally, add the minced parsley.

3 In the meantime, bring a large quantity of salted water to boil in a pot, and cook the bavette until al dente. Place in a frying pan with 2–3 tablespoons cooking water. Add the butter, softened to room temperature, mix well and add the bacon, mushrooms and egg yolks beaten with the red pepper.

4 Place on the fire for a few minutes, mix quickly to blend the ingredients and serve immediately in the pan, sprinkling with grated parmesan cheese.

PRACTICAL SUGGESTIONS
This preparation is a variation of the traditional "spaghetti alla carbonara," a typical dish from the Lazio region that has now spread throughout Italy. The addition of mushrooms will make it more tasty and flavorful.

Tagliatelle with Butter, Sage and Walnuts

INGREDIENTS

serves 4

For the pasta
2 1/4 cups – 250 g FLOUR
2 EGGS
SALT to taste

Seasoning
3/4 to 1 cup – 200 g WALNUTS
1/4 cup – 50 g BUTTER
2 sprigs SAGE
6 tablespoons GRATED PARMESAN CHEESE
SALT to taste

EQUIPMENT
pot
food grinder
small frying pan
rolling pin

Difficulty	EASY
Preparation Time	10 MIN.
Cooking Time	15 MIN.
Method of cooking	STOVETOP
Microwave	NO
Freezing	NO
Keeping Time	1 DAY

SPECIAL NOTE

Unripe walnuts with the hull are the basis for *nocino*, a liqueur that is still prepared in many homes. The walnuts are gathered on June 24, St. John the Baptist's feast day.

RECOMMENDED WINES
Colli Morenici Mantovani del Garda rosato (Lombardy):
rosé served at 57°F / 14°C
Colli Piacentini Ortrugo (Emilia–Romagna):
dry white wine served at 50°F / 10°C

❖

1 Place the flour on the pastry board and break an egg in the center. Add a pinch of salt and, using a fork, mix the ingredients slowly, then knead and work vigorously for 15 minutes until the dough is firm. Shape it into a ball, wrap in a damp cloth and let it rest in a cool place for about 30 minutes.

2 After the dough has rested, take it out and roll it into a thin sheet. Fold it over itself three times and cut it into thin strips about 1/4 inch / 1 cm wide. Spread out on a dish towel and allow to dry for a couple of hours. Bring 1 1/2 quarts / 2 liters of water to boil, salt it, add the tagliatelle and cook al dente.

3 In the meantime, grind the nutmeats in the food grinder. Place the butter in the small frying pan, melt it, add the washed, dried sage, and brown.

4 Drain the pasta and season with the butter and sage, grated parmesan and ground nuts. Serve hot.

PRACTICAL SUGGESTIONS
Instead of homemade tagliatelle, you can use a ready–made pasta in whatever form you prefer, provided it is long. For example, fusilli are also excellent.

Hay, Straw and Peas

INGREDIENTS

serves 4

2 tablespoons — 20 g BUTTER
1 sprig SAGE
4 tablespoons CREAM
1 1/4 cup — 200 g shelled PEAS
SALT to taste
5 oz. — 150 g GREEN TAGLIATELLE
5 oz. — 150 g YELLOW TAGLIATELLE
4 oz. — 100 g HAM
3 tablespoons GRATED PARMESAN CHEESE

EQUIPMENT

a saucepan, preferably earthenware
pot
serving dish

Difficulty	AVERAGE
Preparation Time	10 MIN.
Cooking Time	25 MIN.
Method of cooking	STOVETOP
Microwave	NO
Freezing	NO
Keeping Time	1 DAY

SPECIAL NOTE

Paglia e fieno ("hay and straw") is the name of a combination of green (prepared with spinach) and regular egg tagliatelle. The name comes from the contrasting colors of the two types of pasta.

RECOMMENDED WINES
Martina Franca (Puglia): dry white wine served at 50°F / 10°C
Vernaccia di San Gimignano (Tuscany):
mellow, aromatic white wine served at 50°F / 10°C

1 Place the butter and washed, dried sage into a saucepan, brown a few minutes, then add the cream and finally the peas. Continue cooking for about 15 minutes or until the peas are cooked. If necessary, add a few tablespoons of warm water.

2 Bring a large quantity of salted water to boil in a pot and add the tagliatelle, cooking al dente. In the meantime, cut the ham into strips.

3 When the pasta is cooked, drain and place into a serving dish, add the ham and the sauce and sprinkle with grated parmesan. Mix well, blending the ingredients, and serve immediately.

PRACTICAL SUGGESTIONS
If you like a slightly acidic taste, you can substitute plain yogurt for the cream. If you're in a hurry, you can also add frozen peas rather than fresh ones.

Green Tagliatelle with Corned Tongue

RECOMMENDED WINES
Colli Euganei Merlot (Veneto): light red wine served at 61°F / 16°C
Sangiovese di Romagna (Emilia–Romagna):
light red wine served at 61°F / 16°C

1 Bring a large quantity of salted water to boil in a pot, add the tagliatelle and cook al dente.

2 In the meantime, place the cream, chopped butter, grated parmesan, tongue sliced into strips, a dot of vegetable extract and a pinch of salt and freshly ground pepper into a large saucepan. Cook for a few minutes over moderate heat, mixing with a wooden spoon.

3 When the pasta is cooked, drain it, place on a serving dish and mix to blend the ingredients thoroughly. Sprinkle with minced parsley and serve.

INGREDIENTS
serves 4

1 lb. – 350 g GREEN TAGLIATELLE
1 cup – 2 dl CREAM
1/4 cup – 60 g BUTTER
3 tablespoons GRATED PARMESAN cheese
4 oz. – 100 g CORNED TONGUE SLICED
not too thinly
VEGETABLE EXTRACT (such as Marmite or
Vegemite) to taste
SALT and PEPPER to taste
1 teaspoon minced PARSLEY

EQUIPMENT
pot
saucepan
serving dish

Difficulty	**AVERAGE**
Preparation Time	**10 MIN.**
Cooking Time	**15 MIN.**
Method of cooking	**STOVETOP**
Microwave	**NO**
Freezing	**NO**
Keeping Time	**1 DAY**

PRACTICAL SUGGESTIONS
You may substitute the parsley with finely minced chives or use other types of pasta, preferably long. Condensed beef bouillon may be used in place of vegetable extract. Follow this first course with a low protein, low calorie main dish.

SPECIAL NOTE
Corned tongue is prepared by treating it with a special mix of salt and potassium nitrate. Along with the so-called *bagnetto verde*, it is a classic element of Piedmont hors d'oeuvres.

Roman–Style Tagliatelle

INGREDIENTS

serves 4

1 tablespoon minced PARSLEY
1.5 oz. – 40 g WALNUTS
pinch of MARJORAM
1 scant cup – 200 g ROMAN RICOTTA
2 tablespoons GRATED PECORINO CHEESE
1 lb. – 350 g TAGLIATELLE
SALT and PEPPER to taste

EQUIPMENT

pot
bowl

Difficulty	EASY
Preparation Time	15 MIN.
Cooking Time	10 MIN.
Method of cooking	STOVETOP
Microwave	NO
Freezing	NO
Keeping Time	1 DAY

SPECIAL NOTE

Roman ricotta is prepared by the same dairymen who prepare pecorino cheese. By reboiling the whey and adding a special rennet, they obtain a soft mass with a delicate flavor.

RECOMMENDED WINES
Colli Albani (Lazio): dry white wine served at 50°F / 10°C
Franciacorta bianco (Lombardy): dry white wine served at 50°F / 10°C

❖

1 Trim the parsley, removing the stems, wash, mince finely and place in a bowl with the coarsely chopped walnuts, the marjoram, the ricotta and the grated pecorino. Mix vigorously with a wooden spoon until it becomes foamy and soft.

2 Boil a large quantity of salted water in a pot, add the tagliatelle and cook al dente.

3 Just before draining the tagliatelle, remove a few spoonfuls of cooking water, add to the ricotta mixture, adjust the salt and pepper to taste, and mix the seasoning again. Drain the tagliatelle into the bowl, mix everything thoroughly and serve immediately.

PRACTICAL SUGGESTIONS
Other types of long pasta can be used for this seasoning, which you can change as you like by using other aromatic herbs (for example, thyme or tarragon), or else substituting almonds or pine nuts for the walnuts.

Whole–Wheat Tagliatelle with Herbs

INGREDIENTS

serves 4

For the pasta

1 handful BASIL leaves

1 handful PARSLEY leaves

a few SAGE leaves

1 sprig ROSEMARY

4 1/3 cups – 500 g WHOLE–WHEAT FLOUR

2 EGGS

1 teaspoon EXTRA VIRGIN OLIVE OIL

1 /2 cup LUKEWARM WATER

SALE and PEPPER to taste

Seasoning

TOMATO and BASIL SAUCE

or melted BUTTER

EQUIPMENT

pasta machine

pot, soup tureen

Difficulty	AVERAGE
Preparation Time	30 MIN. + 20 MIN.
Cooking Time	5 MIN.
Method of cooking	STOVETOP
Microwave	NO
Freezing	NO
Keeping Time	3 DAYS

SPECIAL NOTE

The most aromatic basil leaves are those collected before flowering; around this time, there are more aromatic oily substances in the plant.

RECOMMENDED WINES
Valdadige rosato: (Veneto) rosé served at 57°F / 14°C
Ischia rosso (Campania): light red wine served at 61°F / 16°C

1 Trim, wash and thoroughly dry the basil, parsley, sage and rosemary, then use a chopping knife to mince them finely.

2 Place the flour in a mound on the cutting board. Crack the egg into it and add the oil, lukewarm water, a pinch of salt and freshly ground pepper and the minced herbs. Mix all ingredients well and make a dough, working vigorously and keeping the cutting board well–floured.

3 When the dough is quite soft and elastic, form it into a ball, place it on a plate and cover it with a cloth. Let it rest for 15–20 minutes, preferably in the refrigerator, then take it out and divide it into three equal parts. Place it in the pasta machine and select the size for the tagliatelle.

4 Bring a large quantity of water to boil in a pot, salt it and cook the pasta al dente. Drain and place it in a soup tureen, then season to taste with tomato and basil sauce or melted butter.

PRACTICAL SUGGESTIONS

Thus prepared, the tagliatelle will be excellent with many other types of seasonings, for example sautéed vegetables, olive paste, squash and ricotta, and walnut sauce.

Tagliatelle with Poppy Seeds

INGREDIENTS

serves 4

1/4 cup — 60 g SHELLED ALMONDS
SALT to taste
11 oz. — 300 g TAGLIATELLE
3 tablespoons SESAME SEED OIL
2 tablespoons POPPY SEEDS

EQUIPMENT

a small skillet
a pot
a wide saucepan
serving dish

Difficulty	**EASY**
Preparation Time	**15 MIN.**
Cooking Time	**10 MIN.**
Method of cooking	**STOVETOP**
Microwave	**NO**
Freezing	**NO**
Keeping Time	**1 DAY**

SPECIAL NOTE

In Italy, poppy seeds are traditionally used in several regions, such as Trentino, where they are added to the filling for *casunziei*, a sort of ravioli seasoned with beets and potatoes.

RECOMMENDED WINES
Freisa d'Asti secco (Piedmont): light red wine served at 61°F / 16°C
Montecarlo rosso (Tuscany): full–bodied red wine served at 61°F / 16°C

1 Boil water in a small skillet, add the almonds and barely scald them. Take them between your thumb and index finger and pop them out of the skin. After they have all been cleaned, dry them well and sliver them.

2 Bring a large quantity of salted water to boil in a pot, add the tagliatelle and cook them al dente.

3 In the meantime, heat the oil in a wide saucepan, add the almonds and poppy seeds and sauté briefly.

4 When the tagliatelle are cooked, drain and place them into the saucepan with the almonds, add a pinch of salt and mix gently with a wooden spoon, continuing to cook for two more minutes. Transfer to a warm serving dish and serve immediately.

PRACTICAL SUGGESTIONS
Poppy seeds will keep for months if they are well–dried and stored in a glass or ceramic jar with a hermetic seal. Nevertheless, before using them, always make sure they are fresh, or they could give the dish a rancid taste.

Spaghetti alla Versiliese

INGREDIENTS

serves 4

1 lb. — 400 g SMALL FRY FISH
1 handful PARSLEY leaves
2 cloves GARLIC
1 ONION
1 LEEK
1/2 cup EXTRA VIRGIN OLIVE OIL
2 tablespoons TOMATO PUREE
SALT to taste
1 lb. — 400 g SPAGHETTI

EQUIPMENT

a fine strainer
a saucepan
a pot
a soup tureen

Difficulty	AVERAGE
Preparation Time	15 MIN.
Cooking Time	1 HOUR 45 MIN.
Method of cooking	STOVETOP
Microwave	YES
Freezing	NO
Keeping Time	1 DAY

SPECIAL NOTE

Fish is highly nutritious; 3.3 lb. / 1500 g is the equivalent of 2.7 lb. / 1200 g of beef. Ray and mackerel are the most protein–rich.

RECOMMENDED WINES
Pomino bianco (Tuscany): light red wine served at 50°F / 10°C
Bianco di Custoza (Veneto): dry white wine served at 50°F / 10°C

1 Wash the fish well, clean it, bone it and chop into pieces. Mince the parsley, garlic, onion and leek (only the white part) and sauté in oil in a saucepan. When the onion turns golden brown, add the fish cook 2 minutes, then add the tomato puree.

2 Cover with hot water, adjust the salt, cover and cook over low heat for an hour and a half. When the sauce has boiled down, put everything through the fine strainer to obtain a thick sauce.

3 Boil a large quantity of salted water in a pot, add the spaghetti and drain when cooked al dente. Place into the soup tureen and season with the sauce. Serve immediately, garnishing with several sprigs of the remaining minced parsley.

PRACTICAL SUGGESTIONS
You can use many types of small fish for this exquisite spaghetti, including sardines, mullet, and anchovies. If you're in a hurry, use a blender rather than the strainer to make a very thick sauce.

Country—Style Bucatini

INGREDIENTS

serves 4

5 oz. — 150 g CANNELLINI BEANS
I BAY LEAF
2 sprigs ROSEMARY
SALT to taste
3 oz. — 80 g SMOKED BACON in one piece
I ONION
I clove GARLIC
I SAGE leaf
I handful PARSLEY leaves
4 tablespoons EXTRA VIRGIN OLIVE OIL
I RED PEPPER
3/4 lb. — 350 g BUCATINI SPAGHETTI
2 tablespoons GRATED PECORINO CHEESE

EQUIPMENT

I bowl, 2 saucepans
I pot

Difficulty	**AVERAGE**
Preparation Time	**15 MIN. + 12 HOURS**
Cooking Time	**I HOUR 30 MIN.**
Method of cooking	**STOVETOP**
Microwave	**NO**
Freezing	**NO**
Keeping Time	**I DAY**

SPECIAL NOTE

Bucatini, a large spaghetti with a hole down the middle that is typical of the Lazio region, is the smallest spaghetti of its category, which includes perciatelli, mezzanelli, mezzani, zite and zitoni, in order of increasing size.

RECOMMENDED WINES
Valpolicella (Veneto): light red wine served at 61°F / 16°C
Colli Martani Sangiovese (Umbria): light red wine served at 61°F / 16°C

I Wash the beans, place in the bowl and soak in a generous amount of cold water for 12 hours. Drain and run under cold water. Place in a saucepan, cover with a generous amount of water, add the bay leaf and a sprig of rosemary, bring to a boil and cook for about an hour over very low heat, adding hot water if necessary and salting them about halfway through the cooking.

2 In the meantime, cut the bacon into strips. Remove the skin form the onion and garlic, wash and chop them with the other sprig of rosemary, the sage and a little of the parsley.

3 Place the oil, red pepper, minced onion and garlic and herbs into a saucepan and sauté until wilted but not browned. Add the strips of bacon and sauté briefly, mixing with a wooden spoon. Add the cooked, drained beans, cover the saucepan and continue cooking for about 10 minutes over moderate heat.

4 Bring a generous amount of salted water to boil in a pot and cook the bucatini. Drain when al dente, remove the red pepper and season with the bean sauce. Serve the bucatini hot, sprinkling them with the rest of the washed, minced parsley and the grated pecorino.

PRACTICAL SUGGESTIONS
If you want to make this dish but don't have much time, you can substitute canned beans for dry ones, thus eliminating soaking time. The dish will be tastier if you substitute the bacon with lard (from the pig's cheek).

Spaghetti with Asparagus and Almonds

INGREDIENTS

serves 4

4/ 5 lb. – 350 g SPAGHETTI
1/ 4 cup – 50 g BUTTER
1/5 cup – 60 g SLIVERED ALMONDS
1 3/4 cups – 300 g FROZEN ASPARAGUS TIPS
SALT and PEPPER to taste
4 tablespoons GRATED PARMESAN

EQUIPMENT

a pot
a frying pan
a slotted spatula
a bowl
a serving dish

Difficulty	AVERAGE
Preparation Time	15 MIN.
Cooking Time	20 MIN.
Method of cooking	STOVETOP
Microwave	NO
Freezing	NO
Keeping Time	1 DAY

SPECIAL NOTE

Asparagus, which has been cultivated as a prized edible plant since time immemorial, has many common wild varieties, in both temperate and tropical regions.

Recommended Wines
Montecompatri (Lazio): dry white wine served at 50°F / 10°C
Aquileia del Friuli Chardonnay:
mellow, aromatic white wine served at 50°F / 10°C

1 Place a generous amount of water in a pot, salt it and bring to a boil. Add the spaghetti and cook al dente.

2 In the meantime, melt the butter in the frying pan. As soon as it begins to fry, add the almond slivers and brown at low heat. Remove them with the slotted spatula and place them in a bowl.

3 Add the frozen asparagus tips to the butter, being sure that all remaining parts of the white stalk have been removed. Let them cook covered over moderate heat, adding, if necessary, two or three tablespoons of the spaghetti cooking water. Season with salt and freshly ground pepper.

4 Return the slivered almonds to the seasoning, and as soon as the spaghetti is cooked al dente, drain, reserving a small amount of the cooking water, and place into the frying pan. Complete by adding grated parmesan, mix again with a spoon and fork, seasoning everything well, and if necessary, add a tablespoon or two of the pasta cooking water. Transfer to a serving dish and serve.

Practical Suggestions
If you have dried almonds, sliver them as follows: shell them and toss them into a bowl of hot water for a few minutes, then remove the skin, dry them and slice thinly.

Spaghetti with Zucchini

RECOMMENDED WINES
Colli Piacentini Ortrugo (Emilia–Romagna):
dry white wine served at 50°F / 10°C
Bianco delle Colline Lucchesi (Tuscany):
dry white wine served at 50°F / 10°C

1 Place a generous amount of water in a pot, bring to a boil and salt, and then add the spaghetti and cook al dente.

2 In the meantime, trim and wash the zucchini, cut off the ends and cut into rounds. Place the olive oil into a saucepan, preferably earthenware, heat it well and sauté the zucchini, mixing with a wooden spoon and adjusting the salt. Trim the parsley, wash, dry and mince.

3 When the spaghetti is cooked, drain and place in a serving dish. Season with the fried zucchini and frying liquid, sprinkle with minced parsley, mix to season well, and serve immediately very hot. Do not serve with parmesan cheese.

INGREDIENTS

serves 4

3/4 lb. — 380 g SPAGHETTI
4 ZUCCHINI
4 tablespoons EXTRA VIRGIN OLIVE OIL
1 teaspoon minced PARSLEY
SALT to taste

EQUIPMENT

a pot
a saucepan, earthenware if possible
a serving dish

Difficulty	**AVERAGE**
Preparation Time	**15 MIN.**
Cooking Time	**30 MIN.**
Method of cooking	**STOVETOP**
Microwave	**NO**
Freezing	**NO**
Keeping Time	**2 DAYS**

SPECIAL NOTE

The first citation in Italian using the term "spaghetti" to refer to pasta appears in Giacinto Carena's 1846 *Vocabulario domestico*, which, however, equates spaghetti with vermicelli.

PRACTICAL SUGGESTIONS
If you want to add a touch of color to this dish, chop a ripe, peeled tomato with the seeds removed and add it to the zucchini as they cook.

Tagliatelle with Potatoes and Kale

INGREDIENTS
serves 4

For the pasta
2 1/2 cups – 300 g WHITE FLOUR
3 EGGS
SALT to taste

Seasoning
1 lb. – 400 g KALE (or, as it's known in
Italian, Black Cabbage)
over 1/2 lb. POTATOES
4 tablespoons EXTRA VIRGIN OLIVE OIL
2 tablespoons GRATED PARMESAN
SALT to taste

EQUIPMENT
rolling pin
pot
serving dish

Difficulty	AVERAGE
Preparation Time	50 MIN. + 30 MIN.
Cooking Time	20 MIN.
Method of cooking	STOVETOP
Microwave	NO
Freezing	NO
Keeping Time	1 DAY

SPECIAL NOTE
Cabbage is a herbaceous Mediterranean plant in
the Cruciferae family, with many cultivated
varieties. It has an erect stalk and small flowers
in panicles or corymbs.

RECOMMENDED WINES
Colli Tortonesi Cortese (Piedmont):
mellow, aromatic white wine served at 54°F / 12°C
San Severo rosato (Puglia): rosé served at 57°F / 14°C

1 Sift the flour and place it in a mound on the cutting board. Break the egg in the center, add the salt and mix the ingredients by hand until you obtain a soft, uniform dough. Wrap it in a damp cloth and let it rest for about 30 minutes.

2 When the dough has rested, take it out and roll it very thin. Flour the surface, roll it onto itself and using a very sharp knife, cut the tagliatelle to the width of a little less than 1/2 inch (about one centimeter). Spread them on the floured cutting board and let them dry.

3 Clean the cabbage, remove the hard stalks, wash it carefully and cut it into strips. Peel the potatoes, wash and chop into small pieces.

4 Boil a generous amount of water in a large pot, add the potatoes and cabbage, cook for about 10 minutes and then add the tagliatelle. When they are cooked al dente, drain with the vegetables, place in a serving dish, drizzle with olive oil and sprinkle with the grated parmesan. Serve hot.

PRACTICAL SUGGESTIONS
If you're not an expert in preparing homemade pasta (or if you're in a hurry), this recipe will be just as good if you substitute a pound of fresh egg pasta.

Reginette with Red Pesto

INGREDIENTS

serves 4

3/4 lb. — 350 g REGINETTE PASTA
(a type of curled fettucine)
1 tablespoon EXTRA VIRGIN OLIVE OIL
1 dry RED PEPPER
4 tablespoons TOMATO PUREE
5.5 oz. GENOVESE PESTO
GRATED PARMESAN to taste
SALT to taste

EQUIPMENT

a pot
a large frying pan
a serving dish

Difficulty	**EASY**
Preparation Time	**5 MIN.**
Cooking Time	**15 MIN.**
Method of cooking	**STOVETOP**
Microwave	**NO**
Freezing	**NO**
Keeping Time	**2 DAYS**

SPECIAL NOTE

Pesto, which comes from the ancient *agliata* (a
garlic and vinegar sauce), is one of the
fundamental sauces in Ligurian and Provençal
cooking. In Liguria, it is prepared with small—leaf
basil with its delicate fragrance.

RECOMMENDED WINES
Gioia del Colle bianco (Puglia): dry white wine served at 54°F / 12°C
Colli di Luni bianco (Liguria): dry white wine served at 54°F / 12°C

1 Place a generous amount of water in a pot, bring to a boil, salt
and cook the reginette.

2 In the meantime, place the oil in a large frying pan and add the
red pepper. Heat, and a few minutes later add the tomato sauce.
When it has become flavorful, remove the red pepper and add the
Genoese pesto. Mix well to season and cook for 5 minutes, then
remove from heat.

3 Drain the reginette, place directly into the frying pan with the
prepared sauce, season, then place the pasta on a serving dish,
sprinkling generously with parmesan. Garnish with a few basil leaves
if you wish, and serve.

PRACTICAL SUGGESTIONS
*If the sauce is too thick, add a few tablespoons of pasta cooking water. A
fine substitute for the tomato sauce is fresh little Sardinian tomatoes.*

Spaghetti with Almonds

INGREDIENTS

serves 4

1 AVOCADO
juice of half a LEMON
12 ALMONDS
1 tablespoon PINE NUTS
3/4 lb. – 350 g SPAGHETTI
2 tablespoons – 30 g BUTTER
SALT to taste

EQUIPMENT

a bowl
a small skillet
a pot
a small saucepan
a soup tureen

Difficulty	AVERAGE
Preparation Time	20 MIN.
Cooking Time	20 MIN.
Method of cooking	STOVETOP
Microwave	NO
Freezing	NO
Keeping Time	1 DAY

SPECIAL NOTE

Avocados are the fruit of the evergreen avocado tree, a native of Mexico that has spread throughout Latin America, the Antilles, Cameroon and Israel, which are now major producers.

Recommended Wines
Cortese di Gavi (Piedmont): mellow, aromatic white wine
served at 50°F / 10°C
Alcamo (Sicily): dry white wine served at 50°F / 10°C

1 Peel the avocado, which should be properly ripe, i.e., soft to the touch. Cut it in two and remove the stone. Dice it and place it into a bowl, then sprinkle it with the lemon juice to prevent it from turning brown.

2 Boil water in the small skillet, add the almonds and just barely scald them. Use your thumb and index finger to pop them from the skin, then dry them well and mince with the pine nuts.

3 Place a generous amount of water into a pot, salt and boil, then add the spaghetti and cook al dente.

4 In the meantime, melt the butter in a small saucepan, add the almonds and pine nuts and flavor over moderate heat, then add a couple of spoonfuls of pasta cooking water, mix thoroughly again and remove from the stove.

5 Drain the pasta when it is cooked al dente, place into a warm soup tureen, season with the sauce and the dried avocado, mix and serve immediately.

Practical Suggestions
You can tell when an avocado is ripe by testing it as you would a pear; when it's properly ripe, it will give slightly as you press it with your finger.

Spaghetti with Basil

INGREDIENTS

serves 4

4 1/2 oz. – 120 g BASIL
2 tablespoons GRATED PECORINO CHEESE
1 cup EXTRA VIRGIN OLIVE OIL
SALT to taste
1 lb. – 400 g SPAGHETTI
10 hulled WALNUTS

EQUIPMENT

a bowl
a pot
a chopping knife
a serving dish

Difficulty	EASY
Preparation Time	**10 MIN.**
Cooking Time	**10 MIN.**
Method of cooking	**STOVETOP**
Microwave	**NO**
Freezing	**NO**
Keeping Time	**2 DAYS**

SPECIAL NOTE

Basil, which is a member of the mint family, was known to the ancient Greeks. Its name comes from the Greek *basilikón*, royal, and thus means "royal plant."

RECOMMENDED WINES
Cinque Terre (Liguria): mellow, aromatic white wine served at 50°F / 10°C
Capri bianco (Campania): dry white wine served at 50°F / 10°C

1 Trim, clean, wash and dry the basil. Add it to the walnuts and use a chopping knife to chop it very finely. Set aside some of the kernels and basil leaves for garnishing.

2 Place the chopped mixture in a bowl, add the grated pecorino and all the oil, and mix thoroughly with a wooden spoon until the ingredients are well blended and the sauce is creamy.

3 Boil a generous amount of salted water in a pot, then add the pasta, cook, drain and season with the sauce. Transfer it to a serving dish and serve, garnishing with the basil leaves and walnuts you set aside.

PRACTICAL SUGGESTIONS
It is important for this aromatic sauce to be creamy. If it does not appear sufficiently so, add a few spoonfuls of pasta cooking water.

Taglierini Pie

INGREDIENTS

serves 4

1/4 cup — 30 g RAISINS
SALT to taste
1 lb. — 400 g EGG TAGLIERINI
1 sprig ROSEMARY
4–5 leaves SAGE
1/4 lb. GOOSE SALAMI or HAM
8 tablespoons EXTRA VIRGIN OLIVE OIL
1/4 cup — 30 g PINE NUTS
4 tablespoons BREAD CRUMBS

EQUIPMENT

a bowl
a pot
a small frying pan
a cake pan

Difficulty	**AVERAGE**
Preparation Time	**15 MIN. + 20 MIN.**
Cooking Time	**30 MIN.**
Method of cooking	**STOVETOP AND OVEN**
Microwave	**YES**
Freezing	**YES**
Keeping Time	**2 DAYS**

SPECIAL NOTE

At one time, in many regions of Italy, especially the Po Valley, goose was considered a substitute for pork. The meat and part of the fat were even used to prepare salami.

RECOMMENDED WINES
Colli Berici Tocai rosso (Veneto): light red wine served at 57°F / 16°C
Velletri rosso (Lazio): light red wine served at 57°F / 16°C

1 Soak the raisins for 20 minutes in a bowl of lukewarm water. Drain, squeeze and set aside.

2 Heat a pot filled with salted water. When it comes to a boil, add the taglierini and cook very al dente (2–3 minutes).

3 In the meantime, trim the rosemary, wash it and chop with the sage. Cut the goose salami into pieces, and add these ingredients to a small frying pan with 4 tablespoons of olive oil. Fry for 7–8 minutes.

4 When the pasta is ready, drain it and season it with the fried mixture, adding the pine nuts and raisins as well. Grease a cake pan with the remaining olive oil and sprinkle with the bread crumbs. Add the seasoned pasta and bake at about 350° for 20–25 minutes. Remove and serve hot in the baking dish.

PRACTICAL SUGGESTIONS
If you can't find goose salami, this flavorful, very nutritious recipe will be just as tasty if you substitute pork salami. The traditional recipe from Romagna actually used goose ham, which has become a true rarity.

Spaghettoni with Roses

INGREDIENTS

serves 4

11 oz. – 300 g SPAGHETTONI (thick spaghetti)
2 handfuls – 30 g FRESH ROSE PETALS
4.5 oz. – 120 g LEAN COOKED HAM, sliced thinly
1.5 tablespoons – 20 g BUTTER
1 cup CREAM
SALT to taste

EQUIPMENT

a pot
a large frying pan
a deep serving dish

Difficulty	EASY
Preparation Time	10 MIN.
Cooking Time	20 MIN.
Method of cooking	STOVETOP
Microwave	NO
Freezing	NO
Keeping Time	1 DAY

SPECIAL NOTE

Roses are frequently used in the kitchen, especially in pastries. Rose water and rose oil are used to flavor creams, cake batters and sweets or liqueurs, like rosolio, which was once a very common drink.

RECOMMENDED WINES

Erbaluce di Caluso (Piedmont): dry white wine served at 50°F / 10°C
Trentino Chardonnay: mellow, aromatic white wine served at 50°F / 10°C

1 Boil about 2 quarts / 4 liters of water in a pot. As soon as the water comes to a boil, salt it, add the spaghettoni and cook al dente.

2 In the meantime, remove the petals from freshly–cut roses, i possible pink, and wipe them gently with a light, damp cloth, then snip them into pieces, and set about a dozen whole ones aside. Cu the ham into strips and then cubes.

3 Melt the butter in a large pan, fry the ham and add the cream. A soon as it begins to boil, add the snipped rose petals and cook ove moderate heat until the density is correct.

4 Drain the spaghettoni, place in the frying pan and mix well with the sauce, either with a fork or by shaking the pan. Place into a deep warm serving dish, decorate with whole rose petals and serve.

PRACTICAL SUGGESTIONS

This refined, original recipe owes much of its success to its elegan appearance, garnished with rose petals. You should use a pure white undecorated serving dish, or even a dark blue or black dish. Be sure to us fresh, untreated roses from a farmers' market.

Spaghettini with Walnuts and Gorgonzola

RECOMMENDED WINES
Colli Euganei Merlot (Veneto): light red wine served at 61°F / 16°C
Velletri rosso (Lazio): light red wine served at 61°F / 16°C

1 Heat a generous amount of water in a pot. When it comes to a boil, salt it, wait a few moments, then add the spaghettini and cook al dente.

2 Sieve the gorgonzola, place it in a soup tureen and add the vodka and chopped parsley, mixing well with a wooden spoon.

3 Melt the butter in a small saucepan over low heat, but do not fry. Slowly add the gorgonzola until you obtain a smooth, creamy mixture. Finally, add the finely chopped walnut kernels.

4 When the pasta is ready, drain it and place it into the soup tureen with the seasoning. Mix gently to blend the ingredients, then transfer it to a warm serving dish and serve immediately.

INGREDIENTS
serves 4

SALT to taste
3/4 lb. /350 g SPAGHETTINI (thin spaghetti)
8 SHELLED WALNUTS
3 1/2 oz./ 100 g GORGONZOLA
1 tablespoon VODKA
1 tablespoon minced PARSLEY
1/ 4 cup – 50 g BUTTER

EQUIPMENT
a pot
a soup tureen
a small saucepan
a sieve
a serving dish

Difficulty	EASY
Preparation Time	10 MIN.
Cooking Time	15 MIN.
Method of cooking	STOVETOP
Microwave	NO
Freezing	NO
Keeping Time	1 DAY

SPECIAL NOTE
Gorgonzola is aged for 2 to 3 months at 41–46°. During this period, the forms are repeatedly poked with holes to encourage the development of mold.

PRACTICAL SUGGESTIONS
If you don't like the taste of vodka, which is nevertheless quite mild, you can leave it out and substitute it with a tablespoon of rum. But if you want a dish with a much milder flavor, add a tablespoon of pasta cooking water.

With Lemon p72

With Curry p73

With Parsley and Basil p74

With Onions p76

Brianzole p78

With String Bean Cream p80

With Wild Fennel Leaves p82

With Cheese p84

With Green Peppers p85

Short Pasta

Penne with Three Vegetables

INGREDIENTS

serves 6

9 oz. – 250 g GREEN BEANS
11 oz. – 300 g cleaned SPINACH
11 oz. – 300 g SWISS CHARD, cleaned
5 tablespoons EXTRA VIRGIN OLIVE OIL
1 ONION
1 clove GARLIC
SALT and PEPPER to taste
6 PLUM TOMATOES, sliced
6 oz. can – 160 g TUNA IN SPRING WATER
1.5 lb. – 650 g PENNE (short, tubular pasta)
2 tablespoons GRATED PARMESAN CHEESE
2 tablespoons CREAM

EQUIPMENT

2 pots
a frying pan

Difficulty	AVERAGE
Preparation Time	15 MIN.
Cooking Time	50 MIN.
Method of cooking	STOVETOP
Microonde	YES
Freezing	NO
Keeping Time	1 DAY

SPECIAL NOTE

Spinach, Swiss chard and green beans provide protein, sugars, fiber, vitamins and mineral salts, making this dish highly nutritious.

RECOMMENDED WINES
Nuragus di Cagliari (Sardinia): dry white wine served at 50°F / 10°C
Franciacorta bianco (Lombardy): dry white wine served at 50°F / 10°C

1 Trim the green beans, wash and chop into pieces, then cook in boiling salted water in a pot for 10 minutes. Drain. Wash the spinach and Swiss chard, dry and cut into strips that are not too thin.

2 Heat the oil in the frying pan, add the minced onion with the peeled clove of garlic and let the mixture become golden brown. Add the strips of Swiss chard and spinach, mix again, let it wilt, then season with a bit of salt and freshly ground pepper.

3 After a few minutes, add the green beans and slices of tomato. Mix again with a wooden spoon and leave on moderate heat for 20 more minutes. Drain the tuna, crumble it and add it during the last 10 minutes. Mix again and allow the flavors to blend.

4 Cook the penne in a pot with a generous amount of salted boiling water, add them to the pan with the sauce, mix again, sprinkle with grated parmesan and cream, and serve hot.

PRACTICAL SUGGESTIONS
Your guests will appreciate this dish even more if you substitute 7 oz./ 200 g fresh tuna for the canned tuna. Dice it and sauté it in a small non–stick pan with no seasoning.

Penne with Zucchini and Onions

INGREDIENTS

serves 4

SALT and PEPPER to taste
1 lb. – 400 g PENNE (short, tubular pasta)
3/4 lb. – 350 g ZUCCHINI
2 small ONIONS
2 EGGS, 2 tablespoons CORNSTARCH
1/2 cup LIGHT BEER
1 tablespoon MILK
2 tablespoons EXTRA VIRGIN OLIVE OIL
peanut oil for frying
3 tablespoons GRATED PECORINO CHEESE
8 BASIL leaves

EQUIPMENT

a pot, 2 bowls
a frying pan, a slotted spatula
absorbent paper towels
a deep serving dish

RECOMMENDED WINES
Riviera Ligure di Ponente Vermentino (Liguria):
mellow, aromatic white wine served at 50°F / 10°C
Martina Franca (Puglia): dry white wine served at 50°F / 10°C

1 Add a generous amount of water to a pot, bring to a boil, salt, and cook the penne al dente. In the meantime, wash and dry the zucchini, trim them and cut into rounds. Peel the onion, cut into thick rings and leave them under running water.

2 Mix the beaten egg yolks in a bowl and add them to the sifted cornstarch, then gradually add the beer, milk, a pinch of salt and finally the egg whites, beaten to stiff peaks in a separate bowl.

3 Dip the slices of zucchini and onion into the batter one at a time (be sure they are well drained and dry), and brown them in a frying pan in a generous amount of hot oil. As they are ready, remove them with the slotted spatula, place them on absorbent paper towels to absorb any excess grease, sprinkle with salt and keep warm.

4 As soon as the penne are cooked al dente, drain them on a heated serving dish, season with raw olive oil, the grated pecorino, the minced basil leaves and a bit of freshly ground pepper. Add the zucchini and onion slices, mix well and serve.

Difficulty	AVERAGE
Preparation Time	20 MIN.
Cooking Time	30 MIN.
Method of cooking	STOVETOP
Microonde	NO
Freezing	NO
Keeping Time	2 DAYS

PRACTICAL SUGGESTIONS

If you have any leftover batter, you can use it to prepare exquisite savory croquettes, adding pieces of cheese to the batter: use Italico, fontina, Swiss cheese, or even slivers of parmesan.

SPECIAL NOTE

Cornstarch is used as a quick binder to thicken vegetable creams, cooking liquids and vegetable purees.

Penne with Zucchini and Emmental Cheese

INGREDIENTS

serves 4

1 clove GARLIC
1 ONION
1 handful PARSLEY LEAVES
3/4 lb. – 350 g ZUCCHINI
3 tablespoons EXTRA VIRGIN OLIVE OIL
1/2 teaspoon VEGETABLE EXTRACT
1 pinch POWDERED THYME
1 pinch NUTMEG
SALT to taste
1.3 lb. – 500 g PENNE (a short, tubular pasta)
1 tablespoon – 20 g BUTTER
1/2 lb. – 200 g EMMENTAL CHEESE
1/4 cup MILK
1 EGG YOLK

EQUIPMENT

a skillet, a pan
a small saucepan

Difficulty	**AVERAGE**
Preparation Time	**20 MIN.**
Cooking Time	**40 MIN.**
Method of cooking	**STOVETOP**
Microwave	**NO**
Freezing	**NO**
Keeping Time	**2 DAYS**

SPECIAL NOTE

Emmental, the best known of Swiss cheeses, takes its name from its place of origin, the Emmental river valley in the canton of Bern. It made of whole cow's milk, with 45% fat.

RECOMMENDED WINES
San Severo rosato: (Puglia) rosé served at 54°F / 12°C
Colli di Luni rosso (Liguria): light red wine served at 57°F / 14°C

1 Peel, clean and wash the garlic and onion, trim and wash the parsley and mince these ingredients together. Clean the zucchini and chop them into cubes a little less than half an inch (1 centimeter) in size. Place them in a skillet with the oil and minced mixture, and cook for a few minutes. Add the vegetable extract dissolved in a quarter cup of hot water, a bit of thyme and grated nutmeg. Cover and cook at low heat until the zucchini are tender and the sauce has thickened.

2 Place a generous amount of water in a pot, salt it and bring it to a boil, then add the penne and cook al dente.

3 In the meantime, prepare the "fondue." Place the butter in a small saucepan, add the Emmental cheese and melt it over low heat, adding the lukewarm milk. When everything is melted, blend in the egg yolk, continuing to mix and adding a pinch of salt.

4 When the pasta is cooked, drain it and season it with the zucchini sauce and Emmental cream, which should be kept warm in a double boiler. Serve hot.

PRACTICAL SUGGESTIONS
Penne prepared in this way are an excellent one–dish meal, and need only the addition of a fresh vegetable salad or seasonal sautéed vegetables.

Eliche with Mushrooms and Tomato

INGREDIENTS
serves 4

1 lb. – 400 g CULTIVATED MUSHROOMS
2 cloves GARLIC
9 oz. – 250 TOMATOES
or canned plum tomatoes
1 teaspoon MINCED PARSLEY
12 leaves BASIL
4 tablespoons EXTRA VIRGIN OLIVE OIL
1 piece HOT PEPPER
SALT and PEPPER to taste
4/5 lb. – 350 g ELICHE
(a corkscrew–shaped pasta)

EQUIPMENT
1 pot
2 saucepans
a serving dish

Difficulty	AVERAGE
Preparation Time	15 MIN.
Cooking Time	30 MIN.
Method of cooking	STOVETOP
Microwave	NO
Freezing	NO
Keeping Time	1 DAY

SPECIAL NOTE
This recipe uses *geloni (Pleurotus ostreatus)* mushrooms, which grow wild but are now also widely cultivated.

RECOMMENDED WINES
Oltrepò Pavese Pinot grigio (Lombardy):
dry white wine served at 50°F / 10°C
San Severo rosato (Puglia): rosé served at 50°F / 12°C

❖

1 Clean the mushrooms, remove the hard, earthy portion, wash them quickly in cold water, drain, dry and slice. Peel the garlic cloves and crush them slightly. Scald the tomatoes in a pan of boiling water, drain, remove the seeds and vegetable water, then cut into strips.

2 Wash the parsley and basil separately, then dry and chop the basil into thin strips. Wilt the garlic and parsley in a saucepan with two tablespoons of oil, add the mushrooms and sauté over moderate heat for about 3 minutes, mixing from time to time with a wooden spoon.

3 Place the remaining oil in another saucepan and wilt the second clove of garlic with the red pepper. Add the tomatoes, a pinch of salt and pepper and cook over moderate heat for 5 minutes. Add the mushrooms and continue cooking for 5 minutes, mixing from time to time.

4 In the meantime, bring a generous amount of water to boil in a pot. Salt it and cook the eliche. Drain when al dente, season with the mushroom sauce, place in a serving dish and sprinkle with the basil strips. Serve immediately, sprinkling with grated parmesan cheese to taste.

PRACTICAL SUGGESTIONS
The best way to savor the taste of this delicate dish is to use about 7 oz. / 200 g fresh porcini mushrooms instead of the cultivated mushrooms, or 2 oz. / 60 g dried, soaked porcini mushrooms.

Farfalle with Chicken and Pesto

INGREDIENTS

serves 4

1 7 oz. – 200 g CHICKEN BREAST
SALT and PEPPER to taste
4 tablespoons EXTRA VIRGIN OLIVE OIL
1 BAY leaf
leaves from a SPRIG BASIL
leaves from a SPRIG PARSLEY
4 tablespoons DRY WHITE WINE
3/4 lb. – 350 g FARFALLE (bow pasta)
3.5 oz. – 100 g PESTO

EQUIPMENT

a frying pan
a pot
a serving dish

Difficulty	AVERAGE
Preparation Time	10 MIN.
Cooking Time	40 MIN.
Method of cooking	STOVETOP
Microwave	YES
Freezing	NO
Keeping Time	2 DAYS

SPECIAL NOTE

All plants in the genus *Laurus* are poisonous except for the bay laurel, which is used for cooking. If you leave bay leaves in flour or dried fruit, they will keep harmful insects away.

RECOMMENDED WINES
Locorotondo (Puglia): dry white wine served at 50°F / 10°C
Albana di Romagna secco:
mellow, aromatic white wine, served at 50°F / 10°C

1 Clean the chicken breast, wash, dry with a dish towel, and salt and pepper it. In a frying pan, heat the oil and washed and cleaned bay leaf, basil and parsley, add the chicken breast and sauté over high heat until it is completely browned. Remove from the pan and keep it warm between two plates.

2 Pour off the cooking fat, add the white wine and evaporate most of it over high heat. Return the chicken breast to the pan and continue cooking, covered, for 15 minutes over moderate heat, from time to time basting it in the cooking juices.

3 Bring a generous amount of water to a boil, salt it and cook the farfalle. In the meantime, remove the chicken breast from the pan, cut it into strips and place it on the serving dish with the pesto. Drain the pasta, place it in the serving dish, mix well to blend the ingredients, and serve.

PRACTICAL SUGGESTIONS
By gradually increasing the ingredients, this recipe can become an excellent one–dish meal that you can follow with steamed vegetables or a good seasonal vegetable salad. Or, if you like, you can go on directly to the fruit course.

54

Cracked Zite with Mussels

INGREDIENTS

serves 4

2.2 lb. – 1 kg MUSSELS
1 teaspoon MINCED PARSLEY
9 oz. – 250 g SMALL TOMATOES
or tomato sauce
4 tablespoons EXTRA VIRGIN OLIVE OIL
3 tablespoons DRY WHITE WINE
1 clove GARLIC
SALT and PEPPER to taste
1 lb. – 400 g ZITE PASTA
2 tablespoons GRATED SHARP PROVOLONE

EQUIPMENT

a small saucepan
a frying pan
a saucepan
a pot
a serving dish

Difficulty	AVERAGE
Preparation Time	30 MIN.
Cooking Time	25 MIN.
Method of cooking	STOVETOP
Microwave	NO
Freezing	NO
Keeping Time	1 DAY

SPECIAL NOTE

The word cozza comes from southern Italian dialect for mussel *(militi, muscoli or peoci)*, the well—known bivalve mollusk with equal valves, but the word has now become common throughout Italy.

RECOMMENDED WINES

Capri bianco (Campania): dry white wine served at 50°F / 10°C
Martina Franca (Puglia): dry white wine served at 50°F / 10°C

1 Scrub the mussels and wash them repeatedly in a large amount of cold water. Wash the parsley, dry and mince. Heat the little tomatoes in a small saucepan of boiling water, then drain, peel, remove seeds and cut into slices. Allow them to drain another 10 minutes to remove the vegetable water.

2 In the meantime, place the mussels in a frying pan with a tablespoon of oil and wine, add the parsley and keep over high heat until they open. Turn off the heat and remove the mussels from the shell. Strain the cooking liquid and set it aside.

3 Peel the garlic and crush it slightly. Place it in a saucepan with the remaining oil and wilt it. Add the tomatoes, season with a pinch of salt and freshly ground pepper, and cook over high heat for about 5 minutes. Add the mussels and 3 tablespoons of cooking liquid, and cook for 2 more minutes.

4 In the meantime, bring a generous amount of water to boil in a pot, salt it, crack the zite and add them to the water. Drain when al dente, place in the saucepan with the prepared sauce and sauté for a few minutes. Then transfer them to a serving dish, sprinkle with the grated provolone and serve immediately.

PRACTICAL SUGGESTIONS

If you don't like the taste of provolone, this recipe is also excellent if you substitute it with a sprinkling of parsley and grated lemon peel mixed together.

Small Macaroni with Peas

INGREDIENTS

serves 4

3 ONIONS
3 tablespoons EXTRA VIRGIN OLIVE OIL
2 3/4 cups — 500 g SHELLED PEAS (or frozen)
SALT and PEPPER to taste
3/4 lb. – 350 g SMALL MACARONI
1 tablespoon MINCED PARSLEY

EQUIPMENT

a saucepan
a pot
a serving dish

Difficulty	**EASY**
Preparation Time	**10 MIN.**
Cooking Time	**35 MIN.**
Method of cooking	**STOVETOP**
Microwave	**NO**
Freezing	**NO**
Keeping Time	**1 DAY**

SPECIAL NOTE

The Italian word for pea, *pisello*, comes from the Latin *pisum*, which in turn comes form the Greek *pisos, pison*, whose root word means to smash or crush.

RECOMMENDED WINES
Castel del Monte bianco (Puglia): dry white wine served at 50°F / 10°C
Biferno bianco (Molise): dry white wine served at 50°F / 10°C

1 Peel, wash and thinly slice the onion. Place it in a saucepan with the oil and brown it slightly. Add the peas, season them for a minute, then cover them completely with lukewarm water.

2 Place the saucepan over the flame, add a pinch of salt and freshly ground pepper and cook covered over moderate heat until the water has almost completely evaporated and the peas are cooked.

3 In the meantime, place a generous amount of water in a pot, bring to a boil, salt and add the pasta. Cook al dente, then drain and place in a saucepan with the peas. Season them, then place in a heated serving dish, sprinkle with grated parsley and serve.

PRACTICAL SUGGESTIONS
If you like, you can add a teaspoon of minced coriander to give the dish a special flavor. If you add a teaspoon of powdered cumin, it will make the onions more digestible. Instead of macaroni, you can also use other types of short pasta, such as, for example, garganelli (shown in the photo).

Shell Pasta with Squash and Black Olives

INGREDIENTS

serves 4

1 clove GARLIC
1/2 medium ONION
1 sprig ROSEMARY
3 tablespoons SESAME SEED OIL
1 lb. – 400 g SQUASH, cubed
1 ladle VEGETABLE BROTH
SALT and PEPPER to taste
1 tablespoon CAPERS
1.5 oz. – 40 g PITTED BLACK OLIVES
4/5 lb. – 350 g SHELL PASTA
a sprig of PARSLEY leaves
a few BASIL leaves

EQUIPMENT

a frying pan
a pot
a serving dish

Difficulty	AVERAGE
Preparation Time	15 MIN.
Cooking Time	50 MIN.
Method of cooking	STOVETOP
Microwave	NO
Freezing	NO
Keeping Time	2 DAYS

SPECIAL NOTE

Squash is a member of the Cucurbitaceae family. The fruit, which is the edible portion, is a pepo, i.e., it has two fleshy internal parts joined together and a tough outer portion.

RECOMMENDED WINES
Est! Est! Est! di Montefiascone:
mellow, aromatic white wine served at 50°F / 10°C
Cirò bianco (Calabria): dry white wine served at 50°F / 10°C

❖

1 Peel the garlic and onion, trim and wash the rosemary, and use chopping knife to finely mince these ingredients. Place the sesame seed oil in a large frying pan, add the minced mixture and fry.

2 As soon as the mixture begins to turn golden brown, add the cubed squash, mix with a wooden spoon and sauté gently on all sides. Baste occasionally with a spoonful of hot broth and continue cooking over low heat, covered.

3 After cooking about 20 minutes, season with a pinch of salt and freshly ground pepper, and add the capers (rinsed well and drained) and black olives. Mix with a wooden spoon and cook for 10 more minutes.

4 In the meantime, cook the shells al dente in a pot with abundant salted, boiling water, drain and add to the prepared seasoning, mixing thoroughly until it is well–flavored, adding one or two spoonfuls of cooking water. Sprinkle with the minced parsley and basil, transfer to a hot serving dish and serve.

PRACTICAL SUGGESTIONS
If you want to make an excellent one–dish meal, add cubed Emmental or other cheese to the cubed squash, and cook as indicated.

Vegetarian Shell Pasta

RECOMMENDED WINES
Frascati (Lazio): dry white wine served at 50°F / 10°C
Bardolino chiaretto (Veneto): rosé served at 54°F / 13°C

1 Trim the string beans, remove any threads, and wash. Bring a generous amount of salted water to boil in a pot, add the string beans and cook two minutes, then drain and set aside.

2 Chop the tomatoes and wash the peas. Wash the zucchini, trim the tips and cut into thin strips. Trim the carrots, peel, wash and cut these into strips as well. Boil them in salted water for 2 minutes, the drain and set aside.

3 Wilt the thinly sliced onion and peeled, whole clove of garlic in a saucepan with oil, without browning them. Add the zucchini and carrot strips, peas, string beans, a pinch of salt and pepper, and mixing from time to time with a wooden spoon, let the flavors blend for a couple of minutes. Finally, add the tomatoes and continue cooking for 5–20 minutes.

4 Shortly before removing the pan from the heat, wash the basil, dry it and cut into thin strips. Add part of it to the sauce and mix. In the meantime, bring a generous amount of water to boil, salt it and cook the shell pasta. Drain it when it is al dente, season with the sauce and sprinkle with the remaining basil. Serve hot.

PRACTICAL SUGGESTIONS
As the name implies, this recipe is for anyone who eats a vegetarian diet. All you need to do is follow it with a plate of sautéed or steamed vegetables.

INGREDIENTS
serves 4

5 oz. – 150 g STRING BEANS
SALT and PEPPER to taste
7 oz. – 200 g CANNED PLUM TOMATOES
1 cup – 200 g SHELLED PEAS
2 ZUCCHINI
2 CARROTS
1 ONION
1 clove GARLIC
3 tablespoons EXTRA VIRGIN OLIVE OIL
12 leaves BASIL
1 lb. – 400 g SHELL PASTA

EQUIPMENT
a pot
a saucepan

Difficulty	AVERAGE
Preparation Time	30 MIN.
Cooking Time	45 MIN.
Method of cooking	STOVETOP
Microwave	NO
Freezing	NO
Keeping Time	1 DAY

SPECIAL NOTE
The carrot is a herbaceous plant from the Umbelliferae family. The root is the edible portion, and contains aromatic substances in the peel and underlying layers.

Eliche with Rabbit Fricassee

INGREDIENTS

serves 4

3/4 lb. – 300 g TOMATOES
1 ONION
1 CARROT
1 stalk CELERY
2 oz. – 1 handful leaves PARSLEY
2 oz. – 50 g slab BACON
HALF A RABBIT (about 1 1/2 lb. – 600 g)
3 tablespoons EXTRA VIRGIN OLIVE OIL
SALT and PEPPER to taste
1/4 cup DRY WHITE WINE
1.5 oz. – 30 g. DRIED MUSHROOMS
1 BAY LEAF
4/5 lb. – 350 g. ELICHE
(corkscrew–shaped pasta)

EQUIPMENT

a bowl, a pot
a skillet

Difficulty	**AVERAGE**
Preparation Time	**20 MIN.**
Cooking Time	**1 HOUR**
Method of cooking	**STOVETOP**
Microwave	**YES**
Freezing	**YES**
Keeping Time	**2 DAYS**

SPECIAL NOTE

The rabbit is a mammal related to the hare. It is a native of southern Europe and the Mediterranean area of North Africa, but humans have spread it throughout the world.

RECOMMENDED WINES
Franciacorta Rosso (Lombardy): light red wine served at 61°F / 16°C
Rosso Conero (Marche): medium bodied red wine served at 61°F / 16°C

1 Boil the tomatoes in a pot of water for a minute, drain, peel and cut in half. Remove the seeds and vegetable water and dice. Trim and wash the onion, carrot, celery and parsley, and mince. Finely dice the bacon as well, and cut the rabbit into small pieces.

2 Heat the oil in a skillet, add the bacon and minced vegetables and mixing continuously with a wooden spoon, sauté until wilted. Add the washed, dried pieces of rabbit, add salt and pepper, and brown on all sides. Add the wine, evaporate it over high heat, then add the softened, minced mushrooms, the bay leaf and the tomatoes and cook 30 minutes more.

3 When cooked, drain the rabbit pieces, remove the bones and slice the meat into strips. Return them to the sauce after removing the bay leaf, and flavor for 5 minutes.

4 Boil a generous amount of water in a pot, salt it and cook the eliche. Drain them when al dente, add them to the skillet and cover well with sauce. Transfer to a serving dish and serve.

PRACTICAL SUGGESTIONS
To eliminate the typical odor of rabbit, you should let it sit for at least three hours in water acidulated with vinegar and aromatic herbs, then shake it off, wash and cook.

Farfalle with Saffron and Olives

INGREDIENTS

serves 4

1/2 ONION
1 sprig of leaves PARSLEY
1/2 lb.– 200 g BLACK PITTED OLIVES
4 tablespoons EXTRA VIRGIN OLIVE OIL
5 tablespoons DRY WHITE WINE
1 packet SAFFRON
6 tablespoons CREAM
4/5 lb. – 350 g FARFALLE (bow pasta)
6 heaping tablespoons – 100 g GRATED
PARMESAN CHEESE
SALT and PEPPER to taste

EQUIPMENT

a small saucepan
a pot
a small bowl

Difficulty	EASY
Preparation Time	10 MIN.
Cooking Time	20 MIN.
Method of cooking	STOVETOP
Microwave	NO
Freezing	NO
Keeping Time	1 DAY

SPECIAL NOTE

The olive is the fruit of the evergreen olive tree, a member of the Oliceae family, and has been known since at least 3000 BC. The olive is mentioned in the Bible and works by Homer, Herodotus and Virgil.

RECOMMENDED WINES
Vernaccia di San Gimignano (Tuscany):
mellow, aromatic white wine served at 50°F / 10°C
Capri bianco (Campania): dry white wine served at 50°F / 10 °C

1 Peel, trim and wash the onion and parsley. Dry well and use a chopping knife to mince them finely. Place in a bowl. Chop the olives coarsely.

2 Place the oil in a small saucepan over the flame and add the minced onion and parsley. When the onion has wilted, add the olives, sauté for a few minutes, then add the white wine and let it evaporate.

3 Dissolve the saffron in a small bowl with a tablespoon of lukewarm water and a pinch of salt. When the white wine has evaporated, add the cream and the prepared saffron, and mixing with a wooden spoon, blend the ingredients well.

4 In the meantime, bring a generous amount of water to boil in a pot, salt it and cook the farfalle al dente, then drain. Place them in a serving dish, drizzle with the saffron sauce, sprinkle with grated parmesan and a pinch of freshly ground pepper. Mix everything well and serve.

PRACTICAL SUGGESTIONS
If you like the taste of yogurt, you can give this dish a more original flavor by adding the same amount of whole yogurt to the sauce instead of the cream.

Sicilian–Style Pennette

INGREDIENTS

serves 4

2 small EGGPLANTS

1/2 lb. – 200 g FRESH PORCINI MUSHROOMS

3/4 lb. – 300 g TOMATOES

1 clove GARLIC

3 tablespoons EXTRA VIRGIN OLIVE OIL

SALT and PEPPER to taste

2 oz. – 1 teaspoon minced PARSLEY

1 lb. – 400 g PENNETTE (tube–shaped pasta shorter than penne)

2 tablespoons GRATED PECORINO CHEESE

EQUIPMENT

a small saucepan

a saucepan

a pot

Difficulty	**AVERAGE**
Preparation Time	**20 MIN.**
Cooking Time	**45 MIN.**
Method of cooking	**STOVETOP**
Microwave	**NO**
Freezing	**NO**
Keeping Time	**1 DAY**

SPECIAL NOTE

The eggplant, which is a member of the Solanaceae family, is an annual herbaceous plant that is a native of India. The fruit of the same name, which may be purple, yellow or white, is actually a berry.

RECOMMENDED WINES

Colli Albani (Lazio): dry white wine served at 50°F / 10 °C

Colli di Luni bianco (Liguria): dry white wine served at 50°F / 10°C

1 Trim the eggplants, wash and chop into pieces. Remove the earthy part of the mushrooms, wash them quickly and slice. Scald the tomatoes one minute in a small saucepan of boiling water, then remove their seeds, chop into pieces and set aside.

2 Wilt the peeled, lightly crushed garlic in a saucepan with the oil. Add the eggplant and sauté over high heat, mixing often, until browned on all sides. Add the mushrooms and sauté for 2–3 minutes, then drain the eggplant and mushrooms and set aside.

3 Place the tomatoes in the same saucepan, add a pinch of salt and freshly ground pepper and cook over high heat for 15 minutes. Add the eggplant and mushrooms and continue cooking for 5 more minutes. Before removing from the heat, sprinkle with minced parsley.

4 Cook the pasta in a pot with a generous amount of salted boiling water. Drain when al dente, season with the eggplant and mushroom sauce, sprinkle with grated pecorino and serve.

PRACTICAL SUGGESTIONS

If you like, you can garnish the dish with very thinly sliced eggplant sautéed in a frying pan with a bit of extra virgin olive oil and placed on a paper towel to absorb any excess oil.

Trasteverine Penne

INGREDIENTS

serves 4

1 oz. – 25 g DRY PORCINI MUSHROOMS
1 lb. – 400 g FRESH TOMATOES
or canned plum tomatoes
1 ONION
2 oz. – 50 g piece PROSCIUTTO
2 oz. – 2 handfuls PARSLEY leaves
3 tablespoons EXTRA VIRGIN OLIVE OIL
SALT and PEPPER to taste
1 lb. – 400 g PENNE
3 tablespoons GRATED PARMESAN

EQUIPMENT

a bowl
a skillet
a saucepan
a pot
a serving dish

Difficulty	AVERAGE
Preparation Time	15 MIN.
Cooking Time	30 MIN.
Method of cooking	STOVETOP
Microwave	NO
Freezing	NO
Keeping Time	2 DAYS

SPECIAL NOTE

Pasta probably spread to the West through the Arabs. In fact, in Italy, the pasta specialists were the Sicilians, whose cooking was most influenced by Arab cuisine.

Recommended Wines
Frascati superiore (Lazio): dry white wine served at 54°F / 12°C
Oltrepò Pavese rosato (Lombardy): rosé served at 54°F / 12°C

1 Soften the mushrooms by soaking in a bowl with a small amount of lukewarm water. Scald the tomatoes in a skillet of boiling water, then drain, remove the skins, seeds and vegetable water, and put through the strainer. Peel the onion, wash and mince finely. Mince the prosciutto and the washed, dried parsley.

2 In a saucepan with the oil, wilt the onion without letting it brown. Add the prosciutto and briefly sauté, mixing with a wooden spoon, then add the drained, minced mushrooms and season for a minute. Add the tomatoes, season with a pinch of salt and pepper and continue cooking for about 15 minutes, mixing with a wooden spoon from time to time.

3 In the meantime, bring a generous amount of water to boil in a pot, salt it and cook the penne. Drain the pasta when al dente, place it in the saucepan with the prepared sauce, add two tablespoons of pasta cooking water and let it season for a minute.

4 Remove the saucepan from the heat, add the grated parmesan and blend the ingredients. Place the penne in a serving dish, sprinkle with minced parsley and serve immediately.

Practical Suggestions
The excellent flavor of this dish will be fully enhanced if you use 5 oz.– 150 g fresh porcini mushrooms instead of the dried ones. Clean them with a damp cloth and slice thinly.

Macaroni with Green Cauliflower

INGREDIENTS

serves 4

1 lb. – 400 g GREEN PUGLIESE CAULIFLOWER
2 1/2 cups – 300 g DURUM FLOUR
SALT to taste
about 18 oz. – 500 g TOMATO SAUCE
3 tablespoons EXTRA VIRGIN OLIVE OIL
4 tablespoons GRATED PECORINO

EQUIPMENT

2 pots
a slotted spoon
a bowl
a small saucepan
a small metal rod or knitting needle

Difficulty	AVERAGE
Preparation Time	40 MIN. + 1 HOUR
Cooking Time	20 MIN.
Method of cooking	STOVETOP
Microwave	NO
Freezing	NO
Keeping Time	3 DAYS

SPECIAL NOTE

The macaroni used in this recipe from Puglia are created using a special metal tool, and are known as *macarun che fir or minuich.*

RECOMMENDED WINES
Cirò rosato (Calabria): rosé served at 54°F / 12°C
Colli Piacentini Ortrugo (Emilia–Romagna):
dry white wine served at 50°F / 10°C

❖

1 Wash the green cauliflower, break it into florets and boil in a pot of water for about 10 minutes. Drain and keep warm in a covered bowl set on top of the pot with the cooking water.

2 Mound the flour on the cutting board and pour enough lukewarm water in the center to obtain a soft, uniform dough. Work it vigorously for about fifteen minutes, then, taking one piece of dough at a time, shape it into cylinder form about as thick as a finger, and cut it into pieces about 1.25 inches – 3 cm long.

3 Place one piece of pasta at a time on the piece of metal, place your open hands over it and pressing lightly, wind the pasta around the iron. Let the macaroni slip off and fall onto the cutting board. Place the pasta on a dry towel and let it dry for about an hour.

4 Place a generous amount of salted water in a pot and bring to a boil. Add the macaroni and cook for 5–6 minutes, then drain and season with the heated tomato sauce, the coarsely chopped cauliflower florets, the oil and the grated pecorino. Serve hot immediately.

PRACTICAL SUGGESTIONS

If you can't find green Pugliese cauliflower, this recipe will be just as good if you use white cauliflower or (to maintain the final aesthetic effect) broccoli florets instead.

Pennette with Lemon

INGREDIENTS

serves 4

3 large LEMONS
10 tablespoons — 100 g CREAM
2 tablespoons — 30 g BUTTER
SALT to taste
1 lb. — 400 g PENNETTE
(tube–shaped pasta shorter than penne)
GRATED PARMESAN TO TASTE

EQUIPMENT

a mixing bowl
a pot
a serving dish

Difficulty	**EASY**
Preparation Time	**15 MIN.**
Cooking Time	**15 MIN.**
Method of cooking	**STOVETOP**
Microwave	**NO**
Freezing	**NO**
Keeping Time	**1 DAY**

SPECIAL NOTE

After oranges, lemons are the most commonly cultivated citrus fruit in Italy. The plant, which is a native of East Asia, was introduced to the Mediterranean by the Arabs around the year 1000.

RECOMMENDED WINES
Alto Adige Chardonnay: mellow, aromatic white wine served at 50°F / 10°C
Solopaca white (Campania): dry white wine served at 50°F / 10°C

❖

1 Grate the lemon peel (being careful to use only the yellow portion) and place it in a bowl. Add the cream and butter, and using a wooden spoon, mix well to blend the ingredients until obtaining a smooth, uniform sauce..

2 In the meantime, boil a generous amount of salted water in a pot. Cook the pennette al dente, drain and season with the prepared sauce and add a generous amount of grated parmesan. Transfer the pasta to the serving dish and serve hot immediately.

PRACTICAL SUGGESTIONS
It is better to use untreated lemons for this recipe. If you want to add a touch of color to the dish, you can garnish with a sprinkling of minced parsley and a few thin rounds of sliced lemon.

Rigatoni with Curry

Colli di Luni Vermentino (Liguria): dry white wine served at 50°F / 10°C
Bardolino light red (Veneto): rosé served at 54°F / 12°C

❖

1 Peel the onion and slice it thinly. Slice the ham into strips. Trim the parsley, wash it, dry it well and use a chopping knife to mince it (setting aside a few leaves for garnishing).

2 In a large frying pan with olive oil, wilt the onion, add the ham and let it season for a few minutes. Then add the tomato sauce and as soon as it comes to the boil, add the curry. Adjust the salt and cook a few minutes.

3 In the meantime, bring about 2 quarts – 4 liters of water to a boil. Salt it and cook the rigatoni. Drain when al dente, add to the frying pan and mix well with the sauce. Transfer the pasta to a serving dish, sprinkle with parsley, mix one more time, and serve hot, garnishing with the parsley leaves.

INGREDIENTS

serves 4

1 small ONION
4 oz. – 100 g COOKED HAM, in one piece
a handful leaves PARSLEY
3 tablespoons EXTRA VIRGIN OLIVE OIL
6 oz. – 150 g TOMATO SAUCE
1 heaping teaspoon CURRY
SALT to taste
4/5 lb. – 350 g RIGATONI

EQUIPMENT

a pot
a frying pan
a serving dish

Difficulty	**AVERAGE**
Preparation Time	**10 MIN.**
Cooking Time	**30 MIN.**
Method of cooking	**STOVETOP**
Microwave	**NO**
Freezing	**NO**
Keeping Time	**1 DAY**

SPECIAL NOTE

Curry, which is typical of Indian cuisine, is a mixture of various spices. The most common are nutmeg, cloves, mace, cumin seeds, pepper, cardamom and saffron.

PRACTICAL SUGGESTIONS

If you want to use curry in the traditional Indian manner, do this: sauté the onion for a few minutes before adding the sliced ham and tomato sauce. The flavor will be much more pronounced.

Pasta with Parsley and Basil

INGREDIENTS

serves 4

2 oz. – 50 g PARSLEY
2 oz. – 50 g BASIL
1 tablespoon SALTED CAPERS
2 SALTED ANCHOVIES
1 clove GARLIC
6 tablespoons EXTRA VIRGIN OLIVE OIL
SALT and PEPPER to taste
4/5 lb. – 350 g ANY SHORT PASTA

EQUIPMENT

a blender
a gravy boat
a pot
a serving dish

Difficulty	**EASY**
Preparation Time	**20 MIN.**
Cooking Time	**10 MIN.**
Method of cooking	**STOVETOP**
Microwave	**NO**
Freezing	**NO**
Keeping Time	**1 DAY**

SPECIAL NOTE

Basil is an annual plant 8–10 inches – 20–25 cm tall. Originally from Asia, it was highly valued in ancient Indian medicine. When used in large quantities, it can cause a state of euphoria.

RECOMMENDED WINES
Soave (Veneto): dry white wine served at 50°F / 10°C
Riviera Ligure di Ponente Pigato: dry white wine served at 50°F / 10°C

1 Trim and wash the parsley and basil and fully dry them on a clean dishtowel. Remove the salt from the capers and wash the anchovies well under running water to remove all salt, then remove the head and backbone to obtain small filets, which should be broken up coarsely.

2 Place all these ingredients in the blender, add the washed, peeled clove of garlic, the olive oil, a pinch of salt and freshly ground pepper. Blend well and pour the mixture into the gravy boat.

3 Boil a generous amount of water in a pot, salt it and add the pasta. Cook al dente. Drain and place a serving on each dinner plate, adding a bit of prepared sauce in the center. Serve with the remaining sauce in the gravy boar, so each guest can serve himself.

PRACTICAL SUGGESTIONS
For a plate of pasta to be successful, it must be cooked properly. The pot must be large and deep, with edges that are not too high, there must always be a generous amount of water, about a half quart / liter for every ounce of pasta. The water should be salted just as it is coming to the boil (1/ 4 oz. salt for every half quart / liter of water).

Mezze Maniche with Onions

INGREDIENTS

serves 4

3 SALTED ANCHOVIES
1 lb. — 400 g ONIONS
4 tablespoons EXTRA VIRGIN OLIVE OIL
SALT and PEPPER to taste
3/4 lb. — 300 g MEZZE MANICHE PASTA
2 tablespoons GRATED PARMESAN CHEESE

EQUIPMENT

a saucepan
a pot
a serving dish

Difficulty	AVERAGE
Preparation Time	15 MIN.
Cooking Time	45 MIN.
Method of cooking	STOVETOP
Microwave	NO
Freezing	NO
Keeping Time	2 DAYS

SPECIAL NOTE

Onions can be used as a natural medicine as well. For example, they will relieve insect bites, nettle stings and rashes caused by food allergies.

RECOMMENDED WINES
Martina Franca (Puglia) served at 50°F / 10 °C
Colli Albani (Lazio) served at 50°F / 10 °C

❖

1 Remove the salt from the anchovies, wash them well under cold running water, dry them, removes the bones and head and use a chopping knife to chop them.

2 Peel the onions, slice them thinly and place them into a generous amount of cold water. Drain and dry well.

3 Wilt the onions in a saucepan with the oil, without browning them, then add a quarter cup water, flavored with a pinch of salt and a grind of fresh pepper, and continue cooking for about a half an hour in a covered saucepan over moderate heat, mixing occasionally with a wooden spoon. Five minutes before removing from the heat, add the anchovies and mix well.

4 In the meantime, bring a generous amount of salted water to boil in a pot, cook the mezze maniche and drain when al dente.

5 Place the pasta in the saucepan over the heat and add the onion sauce. Mix to blend well. Place it in the serving dish and serve hot immediately, accompanied by grated parmesan.

PRACTICAL SUGGESTIONS
The biggest problem with onions is that they cause the eyes to water when peeling them. To obviate this problem, try to peel them under a faucet of cold running water.

Penne Brianzole

INGREDIENTS

serves 4

1 ONION
2 tablespoons EXTRA VIRGIN OLIVE OIL
1 oz. – 20 g BUTTER
2 oz. – 50 g slab BACON
2 GREEN PEPPERS
18 oz. – 500 g CANNED PLUM TOMATOES
SALT and PEPPER to taste
18 oz. – 500 g PENNE
2 oz. – 50 g FAT TALEGGIO CHEESE

EQUIPMENT

a frying pan
a pot
a soup tureen

Difficulty	**AVERAGE**
Preparation Time	**15 MIN.**
Cooking Time	**40 MIN.**
Method of cooking	**STOVETOP**
Microwave	**NO**
Freezing	**NO**
Keeping Time	**1 DAY**

SPECIAL NOTE

Taleggio is a regional cheese made of whole milk. It is a specialty of northern Italy, in particular Val Taleggio, which is located between Bergamo and San Pellegrino.

RECOMMENDED WINES
Freisa d'Asti (Piedmont) served at 57°F / 14 °C
Breganze rosso (Veneto): red served at 57°F / 14°C

❖

1 Peel the onion, wash it and mince it. Place the oil and butter in a frying pan and heat over medium flame. Add the onion and wilt it over very low heat. Chop the bacon into cubes, add it to the mixture and sauté it very gently.

2 Wash and clean the green peppers, removing the seeds and white internal portions. Chop them into little squares and add them to the cooking ingredients. Mix again and allow the mixture to season over low heat for 5 minutes. Add the tomatoes, crushed with a fork. Mix everything again, add salt and pepper and cook the sauce for 20 minutes over moderate heat.

3 In the meantime, heat a generous amount of water in a pot. As soon as it comes to a boil, salt it and add the penne. Cook al dente.

4 A few minutes before the sauce is ready, cube the taleggio and add it, mixing constantly with a wooden spoon, until it reaches a creamy consistency. Drain the pasta, season it with the prepared sauce and serve hot.

PRACTICAL SUGGESTIONS
Due to the amount of pasta indicated and the high calorie ingredients, this tasty recipe should be served as a one–dish meal that can be followed with a salad of seasonal vegetables or a fresh fruit salad.

Pennette with String Bean Cream

INGREDIENTS

serves 4

3/4 lb. — 300 g STRING BEANS (can be frozen)
SALT and PEPPER to taste
2 EGG YOLKS
1/4 cup CREAM
4 tablespoons GRATED PARMESAN
4/5 lb. — 350 g PENNETTE (a tube–shaped
pasta shorter than penne with lines)
2 tablespoons — 30 g BUTTER

EQUIPMENT

a pot
a vegetable mill
a saucepan
a mixing bowl

Difficulty	AVERAGE
Preparation Time	15 MIN.
Cooking Time	50 MIN.
Method of cooking	STOVETOP
Microwave	NO
Freezing	NO
Keeping Time	1 DAY

SPECIAL NOTE

String beans, also known as green beans, are similar to other beans. The difference is that in string beans, the pod is gathered before it ripens and eaten along with the seeds inside it.

RECOMMENDED WINES
Oltrepò Pavese rosato (Lombardy): rosé served at 57°F / 14 °C
Cirò bianco (Calabria): white served at 50°F / 10 °C

1 Trim the string beans, wash them, and add them to a large pot of boiling, salted water. Cook uncovered. Beat the egg yolks in a bowl, add the cream, the grated parmesan and a pinch of salt and freshly ground pepper. Mix thoroughly to blend everything and set the sauce aside.

2 When the string beans are cooked, use a slotted spoon to remove them from the pan, drain well and run through the vegetable mill. Place the puree in a bowl. Keep the cooking water and use it to cook the pennette al dente.

3 In the meantime, melt the butter in a large saucepan, add the string bean puree and let it season for a few minutes. Add the sauce you set aside, mix again and add the well–drained pasta. Mix quickly, sprinkle with freshly ground pepper and serve immediately.

PRACTICAL SUGGESTIONS
The string bean cooking water can also be used to make a thirst–quenching drink, by adding it to vegetable juices with a squirt of lemon. Refrigerate for several hours before serving.

Penne with Wild Fennel Leaves

INGREDIENTS

serves 4

4 oz. – 2 bunches WILD FENNEL LEAVES
1 lb. – 400 g TOMATOES
5 tablespoons EXTRA VIRGIN OLIVE OIL
1 small ONION
1 clove GARLIC
4 ANCHOVIES IN OIL
SALT and PEPPER to taste
3 oz. BREAD CRUMBS
4/5 lb. – 350 g SMOOTH PENNE
(short, tube–shaped pasta)

EQUIPMENT

a pot
a small saucepan
a frying pan

Difficulty	**AVERAGE**
Preparation Time	**15 MIN.**
Cooking Time	**40 MIN.**
Method of cooking	**STOVETOP**
Microwave	**NO**
Freezing	**NO**
Keeping Time	**2 DAYS**

SPECIAL NOTE

The botanical name for fennel (Foeniculum) comes from the Latin and means hay, in reference to the plant's typical thin leaves (like little rootlets). It was highly valued by the Greeks and Romans.

Recommended Wines
Albana di Romagna secco: dry, served at 54°F / 12 °C
Vermentino di Sardegna served at 50°F / 10 °C

1 Trim the wild fennel, removing the hard portions, then wash it and cook it in a large pot of salted water for 5 minutes. Drain, then set aside the cooking liquid, which will be used to cook the pasta.

2 Scald the tomatoes for about a minute in boiling water, then remove the skin and seeds and mince. In a small saucepan with 4 tablespoons of oil, wilt the minced onion and the crushed clove of garlic. Add the minced anchovies and blend, mixing often. Add the tomatoes, flavor with salt and pepper and cook for 10 minutes, boiling the sauce down a bit. About 5 minutes of cooking, add the previously cooked wild fennel leaves and blend them with the sauce.

3 In the meantime, in a dry frying pan, brown the bread crumbs, turning them often with a wooden spoon. Transfer them to a plate. Add the rest of the olive oil to the pan, place over the heat again with the bread crumbs and season, mixing continuously.

4 Bring the fennel cooking water to a boil and cook the penne. Drain when al dente, season with the fennel sauce and sprinkle with toasted bread crumbs.

Practical Suggestions
If you can't find wild fennel (which is now practically impossible to find on the market), use the leaves of the common fennel, which are less fragrant, or dried fennel seeds.

Sardinian Gnocchetti with Cheese

INGREDIENTS
serves 4

SALT to taste
3/4 lb. – 350 g SARDINIAN GNOCCHETTI
1.5 oz. – 30 g GORGONZOLA CHEESE
1.5 oz. – 30 g TOMA (a whole milk,
semi–cooked cheese)
1.5 oz. – 30 g FRESH RICOTTA
1.5 oz. – 30 g FONTINA CHEESE
1.5 oz. – 30 g NATURAL MOUNTAIN BUTTER
1.5 oz. – 30 g GRATED PARMESAN CHEESE

EQUIPMENT
a pot
a bowl
a serving dish

Difficulty	EASY
Preparation Time	10 MIN.
Cooking Time	20 MIN.
Method of cooking	STOVETOP
Microwave	NO
Freezing	NO
Keeping Time	1 DAY

SPECIAL NOTE
The principal constituent of cheese is paracasein, a protein substance. Soft, fresh cheeses also contain a certain amount of vitamins.

RECOMMENDED WINES
Alto Adige Lagrein rosato: rosé, served at 57°F / 14 °C
Gioia del Colle rosso (Puglia): red served at 57°F / 14 °C

1 Heat a pot of 2 quarts of water (Sardinian gnocchetti are made of durum wheat and require a large quantity of water to cook well), bring it to a boil, add a handful of salt and throw in the gnocchi. Boil for at least 20 minutes.

2 In the meantime, cube all the cheeses (of course, remove any rind that may be present), and place them in a mixing bowl.

3 When the gnocchetti are ready, drain and return to the cooking pot. Add the various cubed cheeses, the butter and the grated parmesan. Mix to blend well and serve in a heated serving dish.

PRACTICAL SUGGESTIONS
This is a very high calorie dish, and thus makes an excellent single–dish meal. You can follow it with a plate of steamed vegetables seasoned with a bit of extra virgin olive oil, or a good fruit salad with fruit of the season.

Ditalini with Green Peppers

1 Rinse the anchovies well, eliminating all salt, then bone them and break into pieces. Wash the green pepper, remove the seeds and white parts and cut it into cubes.

2 Bring a generous amount of water to boil in a pot, salt it and add the ditalini. Cook al dente.

3 In the meantime, brown the peeled, slightly crushed garlic in the oil in the saucepan. Then remove the pan from the heat, add the anchovies and, with the aid of a fork, boil it into a cream. Then add the cubed green pepper and cook for about 10 minutes over moderate heat.

4 When the pasta is cooked, drain it, turn into a heated serving dish, season with the prepared sauce, sprinkle with minced parsley and serve.

INGREDIENTS
serves 4

2 ANCHOVIES IN SALT
I GREEN PEPPER
SALT to taste
3/4 lb. — 350 g LINED DITALINI
(a small, ring–shaped pasta)
I clove GARLIC
3 tablespoons EXTRA VIRGIN OLIVE OIL
minced PARSLEY to taste

EQUIPMENT
a pot
a small saucepan
a serving dish

Difficulty	**AVERAGE**
Preparation Time	**15 MIN.**
Cooking Time	**20 MIN.**
Method of cooking	**STOVETOP**
Microwave	**NO**
Freezing	**NO**
Keeping Time	**2 DAYS**

PRACTICAL SUGGESTIONS
To make this plate more digestible, you can brown the green pepper in a very hot oven or hold it directly over the gas flame with a fork. Cool it in a paper sack for a few minutes, then remove the skin and filaments and cut it into cubes.

SPECIAL NOTE
While they are not particularly rich in nutrients due to their high water content, green peppers are quite important due their high content of ascorbic acid, or vitamin C.

Baked   p112

Royale   p113

Della Val Pusteria   p114

With Vegetable Sauce   p116

With Cardoon Cream   p118

Cooked in Sauce   p122

With Preboggion   p120

Baked and Filled Pasta

Riviera-Style Lasagna

INGREDIENTS

serves 4

8 ARTICHOKES
JUICE OF 1 LEMON
SALT to taste
2 tablespoons EXTRA VIRGIN OLIVE OIL
8 FRESH LASAGNA–TYPE EGG NOODLES
1/4 cup – 50 g BUTTER
1 scant tablespoon – 20 g WHITE FLOUR
1 scant cup – 200 g MILK
NUTMEG to taste
2 handfuls GRATED PARMESAN CHEESE

EQUIPMENT

a mixing bowl, 2 pots
a vegetable mill
a skillet
a slotted spoon, a sifter
a rectangular pan

Difficulty	**AVERAGE**
Preparation Time	**20 MIN.**
Cooking Time	**1 HOUR 10 MIN.**
Method of cooking	**STOVETOP AND OVEN**
Microwave	**YES**
Freezing	**YES**
Keeping Time	**2 DAYS**

SPECIAL NOTE

Lasagna is one of the most ancient forms of pasta, after gnocchi. In fact, lasagna and macaroni both appear in a Florentine chronicle from 1370.

RECOMMENDED WINES
Riviera Ligure di Ponente Vermentino (Liguria):
dry white wine served at 50°F / 10°C
Riviera del Garda chiaretto (Lombardy): rosé served at 57°F/14°C

1 Clean the artichokes, cut into slices and soak in a bowl of water and the juice of half a lemon. Boil water in a pot, salt it and add the remaining lemon juice and the artichokes. Boil 20 minutes, drain and squeeze to remove the remaining water, then put through the vegetable mill and place in a skillet.

2 Place a generous amount of water in a pot, add the oil, salt the water, and when the water comes to a boil, cook the lasagna noodles 2–3 at a time. As soon as they are ready, pull them out with a slotted spoon and place them to dry on a damp dishcloth. Preheat the oven to 400°F.

3 Heat the skillet with the artichoke puree, add the butter, reserving a tablespoon full, sprinkle with sifted flour, season for 5 minutes over moderate heat, and add the milk, stirring continuously. Cook for another 5 minutes. Adjust the salt and sprinkle generously with nutmeg.

4 Butter the baking pan, place 2 lasagna noodles on the bottom, cover with a portion of the artichoke cream, sprinkle with parmesan and continue layering until you have finished the ingredients, ending with the cream and cheese. Bake 20 minutes until the surface is crispy. Let it sit outside the oven for a few minutes, and serve.

PRACTICAL SUGGESTIONS
If you're in a hurry, use 18 oz. – 500 g frozen artichokes instead of the fresh ones. In this case, you will not have to put them in the lemon water.

Lasagna with Ricotta and Walnuts

RECOMMENDED WINES
Franciacorte bianco (Lombardy): dry white wine served at 50°F / 10°C
Montepulciano d'Abruzzo Cerasuolo (Abruzzi): rosé served at 57°F / 14°C

1 Prepare the lasagna noodles: sift the flour into a mound on the cutting board, break an egg into the center, salt it and work the dough well. Form a ball, wrap it in a sheet of aluminum foil, and let it rest about 30 minutes..

2 Prepare the sauce: scald the nuts in boiling water, then remove the skin. Place the nuts, ricotta, 2 tablespoons – 30 g of the parmesan, a little over half (30 g) the butter, the oil, the milk, the peeled, washed garlic and the salt, into the blender, then blend for a few minutes until you obtain a creamy, uniform sauce.

3 Take out the dough and roll it into a thin sheet, flour it and cut it into rectangles. Cook these a few at a time in a pot with boiling salted water and 2 tablespoons oil. As they are cooked, remove with a slotted spoon and dry on a damp dishcloth.

4 Butter a baking pan and place the pasta rectangles in layers, alternating with the walnut sauce (if necessary, thin it with some of the pasta cooking water). Bake at 350°F for about 20 minutes, and serve warm, sprinkling with the remaining parmesan.

PRACTICAL SUGGESTIONS
To make this excellent recipe, you can use 1 lb. prepared fresh pasta noodles instead of homemade pasta. Accompanied with steamed mixed vegetables, it can make an excellent one–dish meal.

INGREDIENTS
serves 4

For the pasta
2 1/2 cups – 300 g WHITE FLOUR
3 EGGS
pinch of SALT
2 tablespoons OLIVE OIL

For the sauce
30 WALNUTS
1 lb. – 400 g ROMAN RICOTTA
4 heaping tablespoons – 80 g GRATED
PARMESAN CHEESE
1/4 cup – 50 g BUTTER
4 tablespoons OLIVE OIL
10 tablespoons MILK
1 clove GARLIC
SALT to taste

EQUIPMENT
a blender, a rolling pin
a pot, a baking pan, aluminum foil

Difficulty	**AVERAGE**
Preparation Time	**30 MIN. + 30 MIN.**
Cooking Time	**40 MIN.**
Method of cooking	**OVEN**
Microwave	**YES**
Freezing	**YES**
Keeping Time	**2 DAYS**

SPECIAL NOTE
The walnut tree (*Juglens regia*) begins to produce nuts when it is 8–10 years old. Its production continues to increase until it is about 40 or 50 years old.

Taglierini Timbales in Phyllo Dough

INGREDIENTS

serves 4

6 oz. – 150 g CARROTS, 6 oz. – 150 g LEEKS
6 oz. – 150 g ZUCCHINI
2 tablespoons – 30 g BUTTER
3/4 lb. – 250 g TAGLIERINI
3 tablespoons GRATED PARMESAN CHEESE
SALT and PEPPER to TASTE
3/4 LB. – 250 G PREPARED PHYLLO DOUGH
1 EGG, half a WHITE TRUFFLE (optional)
1 teaspoon WHITE TRUFFLE cream
1 cup – 2 dl CREAM
For the béchamel
1 oz. – 25 g BUTTER
1 level tablespoon – 25 g WHITE FLOUR
1 cup – 3 dl MILK, SALT and PEPPER to taste
pinch of NUTMEG

EQUIPMENT

a skillet, a saucepan, 2 small saucepans
a mixing bowl, a pot, a rolling pin
a baking sheet

Difficulty	**ELABORATE**
Preparation Time	**30 MIN.**
Cooking Time	**1 HOUR**
Method of cooking	**STOVETOP AND OVEN**
Microwave	**YES**
Freezing	**NO**
Keeping Time	**2 DAYS**

SPECIAL NOTE

The truffle is a mushroom with a subterranean fruiting body in the form of a tuber. Because of its particular, very strong odor, it can be located by specially-trained dogs.

RECOMMENDED WINES
Colli Piacentini Barbera (Lombardy): light red wine served at 61°F / 16°C
Dolcetto delle Langhe Monregalesi (Piedmont): light red wine served at 61°F / 16°C

1 Clean and wash the vegetables. Cut into strips and scald them separately in a skillet of salted boiling water. Drain and sauté for 3–4 minutes in a saucepan with the butter and a pinch of salt and pepper.

2 Melt the butter in a small saucepan, add the flour and sauté. Pour in the milk, season with salt, pepper and nutmeg, and stirring often, cook for 10 minutes. Pour the béchamel into a bowl, add the prepared vegetables, the truffle cream, and blend everything.

3 Cook the taglierini in a pot of boiling salted water. Drain when al dente, add to the mixture and mix gently, adding the parmesan and a pinch of salt and pepper. Roll the phyllo dough into a thin sheet, cut it into squares about 5 inches – 12 centimeters in length, place some of the prepared filling in the center, and seal, forming little bundles. Brush with slightly beaten egg, place on a lightly moistened baking sheet, and bake about 15 minutes at 350°.

4 Scrub the truffle, wash it quickly and cut into thin slices. Place the cream into a small saucepan and reduce it by about half over medium heat. Add the truffle slices and heat. Serve the little timbales hot, with the prepared sauce.

PRACTICAL SUGGESTIONS
You can also use the less expensive black truffles or Norcia truffles for this recipe, or else canned truffles, but you will lose the special fragrance of white truffles.

Lasagna with Artichokes and Spinach

INGREDIENTS

serves 4

3/4 lb. – 300 g FRESH EGG PASTA
4 ARTICHOKES
1 1/8 lb. – 500 g SPINACH
1 tablespoon LEMON JUICE
1 level tablespoon – 25 g WHITE FLOUR
1/3 cup – 75 g BUTTER
1 cup – 3 dl MILK
3 tablespoons GRATED PARMESAN
pinch of NUTMEG
2 tablespoons OLIVE OIL
SALT and PEPPER TO TASTE

EQUIPMENT

a bowl, a frying pan
a saucepan, a small saucepan
a pot, a baking pan

Difficulty	**ELABORATE**
Preparation Time	**1 HOUR + 30 MIN.**
Cooking Time	**1 HOUR**
Method of cooking	**STOVETOP AND OVEN**
Microwave	**YES**
Freezing	**YES**
Keeping Time	**3 DAYS**

SPECIAL NOTE

The substance that makes artichokes so important for our health is cynarin, an alkaloid that helps the liver remove toxins from the body.

RECOMMENDED WINES
Capriano del Colle Trebbiano (Lombardy):
dry white wine served at 57°F / 12°C
Colli Berici Pinot bianco (Veneto): dry white wine served at 50°F / 10°C

❖

1 Clean the artichokes, cut into thin slices and place into a bowl with water and the lemon juice. Trim the spinach, wash well in cold water, drain and cut into strips. Sauté in a frying pan with 2 tablespoons – 20 g butter for 3 minutes. Salt and pepper. Drain the artichokes and sauté in a saucepan with 2 tablespoons – 20 g butter, add 2–3 tablespoons water, salt and pepper, and continue cooking for 10 minutes over moderate heat in a covered saucepan. Melt 2 tablespoons – 25 g butter in a small saucepan, add the flour and sauté for 2 minutes. Add the milk and bring to a boil. Season with salt, pepper and nutmeg, and continue cooking for 10 minutes. Remove the saucepan from the heat and, stirring, add the spinach strips and slices of artichoke (setting some aside for garnishing).

2 Roll the pasta and cut out disks 4 inches – 10 centimeters in diameter. Cook them a few at a time in a pot of salted boiling water and two tablespoons oil. Drain and dip into cold water for a moment, drain again and place on a damp dishtowel. Brush a baking pan with the remaining butter, arrange the disks of pasta in it, forming 2 or 3 layers, alternating with the spinach and artichoke mixture and a pinch of grated parmesan. Spread some of the mixture on the last layer, and place the slices of artichoke you had set aside on top. Bake for 10 minutes at 350°F until browned, and serve.

PRACTICAL SUGGESTIONS

Even if you're in a hurry, you can still prepare this dish by using frozen spinach and artichokes instead of fresh. This way, you'll avoid the vegetable preparation stage.

Baked Pasta with Meatballs

INGREDIENTS

serves 4

1 lb. – 400 g GROUND PORK
1/2 lb. – 200 g GRATED PECORINO CHEESE
2 EGGS, SALT and PEPPER to taste
1 cup EXTRA VIRGIN OLIVE OIL
3/4 lb. – 300 g FRESH LASAGNA–TYPE
EGG NOODLES
1 1/2 lb. – 600 G TOMATO SAUCE
with GARLIC, OREGANO and CAPERS
4 HARD–BOILED EGGS, sliced
1/2 lb.– 200 g PROVOLONE, cubed

EQUIPMENT

a bowl
a frying pan
a pot, a saucepan
a baking dish
absorbent paper towels

Difficulty	**AVERAGE**
Preparation Time	**30 MIN.**
Cooking Time	**50 MIN.**
Method of cooking	**STOVETOP AND OVEN**
Microwave	**YES**
Freezing	**YES**
Keeping Time	**2 DAYS**

SPECIAL NOTE

In the fourteenth century, eggs were cooked in ways that gradually fell into disuse: under the coals, grilled, or scrambled, sweetened and spiced as a filling for fried ravioli.

RECOMMENDED WINES
Montepulciano d'Abruzzo (Abruzzi): light red wine served at 61°F / 16°C
Cirò rosé (Calabria): rosé served at 57°F / 14°C

1 Place the meat in a bowl with about 4 heaping tablespoons – 80 g pecorino, the two eggs, a pinch of salt and one of freshly ground pepper. Mix the ingredients with a wooden spoon, and use your hands to shape many small meatballs, about as big as an olive.

2 Heat the oil in a frying pan (reserving two tablespoons) and fry the meatballs. When they have browned, remove them and place them on paper towels to absorb the excess grease.

3 Place the remaining oil in a pot, add a generous amount of water, and as soon as it comes to a boil, salt it and cook the lasagna noodles. Remove them as they are done and place them on a damp dishtowel. Preheat the oven to 350°F.

4 Heat the tomato sauce in a small saucepan, then add a few spoonfuls to a baking dish, add a layer of noodles, another layer of sauce, some of the meatballs, some slices of hardboiled egg, part of the provolone and part of the pecorino. Continue to form layers until you have finished the ingredients. Finish with a sprinkling of grated pecorino and bake for 30 minutes. Serve the lasagna in the baking dish.

PRACTICAL SUGGESTIONS
If the meatball mixture is too soft, add a few tablespoons fine bread crumbs. The original recipe also calls for the addition of pieces of sausage and ricotta.

Baked Rigatoni, Pugliese Style

INGREDIENTS

serves 4

1 lb. – 400 g RIGATONI
1 lb. – 400 g PLUM TOMATOES
EXTRA VIRGIN OLIVE OIL to taste
1 handful leaves PARSLEY
2 cloves GARLIC
2 tablespoons – 30 g GRATED PECORINO
SALT and PEPPER TO TASTE

EQUIPMENT

a baking dish
a pot

Difficulty	**EASY**
Preparation Time	**10 MIN.**
Cooking Time	**30 MIN.**
Method of cooking	**STOVETOP AND OVEN**
Microwave	**YES**
Freezing	**NO**
Keeping Time	**2 DAYS**

SPECIAL NOTE

Pecorino is a hard, cooked cheese with a typically grayish white color. It is made exclusively from whole sheep's milk processed with lambsmilk rennet.

RECOMMENDED WINES
San Severo rosato (Puglia): rosé served at 54°F / 12°C
Lambrusco di Sorbara (Emilia–Romagna): light red wine served at 57°F / 14°C

1 First of all, preheat the oven to 350°F. Wash the tomatoes and cut them into rounds of the same thickness. Remove the seeds and place the tomatoes on the bottom of an oiled baking dish until they completely cover it.

2 Wash and trim the parsley, peel the garlic and chop them coarsely. Place a pot with a generous amount of water on the heat and cook the rigatoni very al dente.

3 Drain, place the pasta in the baking dish on top of the tomatoes. Sprinkle everything with the minced garlic and parsley and the grated pecorino, and drizzle with two tablespoons of oil. Salt and pepper and then bake for 20 minutes. Serve warm in the baking dish.

PRACTICAL SUGGESTIONS

If your oven does not have a thermostat and you don't know how to tell the temperature, do this: place a sheet of white paper in the oven and close the door. After a minutes, check the color of the paper. If it is light, the heat is moderate, if it is dark, the oven is about 400°, and if it is dark brown, the oven is extremely hot. Be careful: do not let the paper burn!

Fried Ravioli with Squash and Beans

INGREDIENTS

serves 4

1 3/4 cups — 200 g WHITE FLOUR

2 oz. — 50 g RICE

1 clove GARLIC

2 sprigs PARSLEY

2 sprigs MARJORAM

18 oz. — 500 g SQUASH

1/2 lb. — 100 g CANNED CANNELLINI BEANS

3 tablespoons GRATED PARMESAN

1 tablespoon GRATED PECORINO

2 EGGS

2 tablespoons EXTRA VIRGIN OLIVE OIL

SALT and PEPPER to taste

PEANUT OIL for frying

EQUIPMENT

2 bowls, a pot, a saucepan
a baking pan, a potato ricer, a rolling pin
a frying pan, absorbent paper towels

Difficulty	**AVERAGE**
Preparation Time	**30 MIN. + 13 HOURS**
Cooking Time	**2 HOURS 10 MIN.**
Method of cooking	**STOVETOP AND OVEN**
Microwave	**NO**
Freezing	**NO**
Keeping Time	**1 DAY**

SPECIAL NOTE

The word farina ("flour" in Italian) goes back to ancient Rome, and is related to the word farro, or spelt wheat, a cereal cultivated in ancient times that later fell into disuse, except in some regional cooking in areas like Tuscany.

RECOMMENDED WINES
Oltrepò Pavese rosato (Lombardy): rosé served at 57°F / 14°C
Cilento rosato (Campania): rosé served at 57°F / 14°C

1 Sift the flour onto the cutting board, add a pinch of salt and enough water to make an elastic, uniform dough. Wrap it in a dishtowel and let it rest in a cool place for about 30 minutes. Preheat the oven to 375°.

2 Cook the rice al dente in a saucepan with boiling water, and drain. Peel and mince the garlic. Trim and wash the parsley and the marjoram, and mince. Cut the squash into pieces, place it in a baking dish and bake 30 minutes. Let it cool and then rice it into a bowl.

3 Crush the beans and add them to the squash. Add the minced herbs, the garlic, the parmesan and pecorino, the rice, the eggs, the olive oil and a pinch of salt and freshly ground pepper and mix everything with a wooden spoon until the mixture is well–blended.

4 Roll the dough into a thin layer and cut it into many small squares about 4 inches – 10 centimeters long. Place a little heap of the mixture in the center of each one, fold up the dough and press the edges well to close them. Fry the ravioli in a frying pan with a generous amount of hot but not boiling peanut oil. Drain them on absorbent paper towels and serve hot.

PRACTICAL SUGGESTIONS
You can use an equal amount of fresh beans instead of canned ones. Soak them in a bowl of cold water for 12 hours, then drain and cook in salted boiling water for about an hour.

Savory Cannelloni

INGREDIENTS

serves 4–6

8 SQUARES OF FRESH PASTA
1/2 ONION, 1 clove GARLIC
4 tablespoons EXTRA VIRGIN OLIVE OIL
1/2 lb. – 200 g UNSPICED SAUSAGE
1/2 lb. – 200 g GROUND BEEF
3 tablespoons – 50 g GRATED PARMESAN
SALT and PEPPER to taste
1 sprig ROSEMARY, 4 leaves SAGE
5 tablespoons DRY WHITE WINE
2 tablespoons WHITE FLOUR
2 tablespoons CREAM, 2 EGGS

For the sauce

1 ONION
3 tablespoons EXTRA VIRGIN OLIVE OIL
18 oz. – 500 g CANNED PLUM TOMATOES
6 leaves BASIL, 1 MOZZARELLA
SALT and PEPPER to taste

EQUIPMENT

a pot, a skillet, a blender
a baking dish, a saucepan

Difficulty	AVERAGE
Preparation Time	30 MIN.
Cooking Time	1 HOUR 20 MIN.
Method of cooking	STOVETOP AND OVEN
Microwave	YES
Freezing	YES
Keeping Time	3 DAYS

SPECIAL NOTE

Sausage is the most ancient type of salami. It is made by inserting a mixture of ground meats into the intestine. The meat is generally pork, but beef or lamb can also be used.

RECOMMENDED WINES
Grignolino d'Asti (Piedmont): light red wine served at 61°F / 16°C
Colli Orientali del Friuli Merlot (Friuli): light red wine served at 61°F / 16°C

❖

1 Bring a generous amount of salted water to boil in a pot and cook the pasta squares. Drain and allow to cool on a dry dishtowel. Preheat the oven to 350°F.

2 Peel the onion and the clove of garlic, mince, place in a skillet with the oil and brown. Add the crumbled sausage and the beef, and sauté. Season with a pinch of salt and pepper. Add the washed and minced rosemary and sage, pour on the white wine and allow to evaporate. Sprinkle with the flour, mix again, add the cream and cook for 10 minutes. Turn off the heat, put the mixture through the blender and put everything into a bowl. Mix in the eggs and parmesan, mix well again and let it cool. Spread the mixture on the pasta squares, roll up and arrange in a lightly oiled baking dish.

3 Brown the onion in a saucepan with the oil, add the tomatoes, season with salt and pepper and reduce for 15 minutes. Add the minced basil. Cover the cannelloni with sauce, sprinkle with the grated mozzarella and bake for 20 minutes. Serve in the baking dish.

PRACTICAL SUGGESTIONS
You can find pasta squares at supermarkets or grocery stores, but if you want to make them yourself, you'll need 3/4 lb. flour, 3 eggs, 1 tablespoon oil, and salt. When the pasta is homemade, the cannelloni are lighter and cook more rapidly.

Green Pepper Cannelloni

RECOMMENDED WINES
Sangiovese d'Aprilia (Lazio): light red wine served at 57°F / 14°C
Rubino di Cantavenna (Piedmont): light red wine served at 61°F / 16°C

1 Place the dry bread crumbs in a bowl and moisten with the milk. Mince the garlic and the onion and cut the green pepper into strips. Place the oil in a saucepan along with half the garlic and onion. When they have wilted, add the green pepper and sauté for a minute. Salt and pepper and continue cooking for 20 minutes. Then put the mixture in the blender, setting aside a few strips of green pepper. In another saucepan, wilt the minced garlic and remaining onion, add the meat and pork loin and sauté. Add the wine and evaporate. Remove from the heat and cool. Pour everything into a mixing bowl, add the beaten mixture, the squeezed bread crumbs, the egg, the parmesan, the nutmeg and the salt, mix and put everything into the pastry bag, then fill the cannelloni. Preheat the oven to 350°F.

2 Wash and mince the onion, scald the tomatoes in boiling water, drain, skin and chop. Place the oil, onion, half the basil, the sage, and the marjoram in a saucepan and cook until the onion wilts. Add the tomatoes, salt, and pepper, and cook for 10 minutes, reducing the sauce. Remove from the heat and put through the food mill, then reheat. Mince the remaining basil and add it. Spread half the sauce on the bottom of a baking dish, place the cannelloni in the dish, cover with the remaining sauce and garnish with the strips of green pepper. Cover with aluminum foil and bake for 30 minutes. Just before it's done, remove the foil and let the top brown. Serve hot.

PRACTICAL SUGGESTIONS

To make these tasty cannelloni easier to digest, before using the green peppers, prepare them as follows: brown them lightly over a high flame (a wood or charcoal fire would be ideal, but a broiler also works), or scald them in boiling water, and then remove the skin.

INGREDIENTS

serves 4

a handful — about 30 g DRY BREAD CRUMBS
1/4 cup MILK, 1 clove GARLIC, 1 ONION
3 tablespoons EXTRA VIRGIN OLIVE OIL
2 GREEN PEPPERS
1/2 lb. — 200 g GROUND BEEF
2 oz. — 50 g GROUND PORK LOIN
5 tablespoons RED WINE, 1 EGG
2 heaping tablespoons GRATED PARMESAN CHEESE
a pinch NUTMEG, SALT and PEPPER to taste
12 CANNELLONI

For the sauce

1/2 ONION, 3/4 lb. — 300 g TOMATOES or
CANNED PLUM TOMATOES
2 tablespoons EXTRA VIRGIN OLIVE OIL
a few leaves BASIL, 1 leaf SAGE
1 SPRIG MARJORAM
SALT and PEPPER to taste

EQUIPMENT

a bowl, 3 saucepans, a mixing bowl, a pastry bag
a pot, a baking dish

Difficulty	**ELABORATE**
Preparation Time	**30 MIN.**
Cooking Time	**1 HOUR 30 MIN.**
Method of cooking	**STOVETOP AND OVEN**
Microwave	**YES**
Freezing	**YES**
Keeping Time	**3 DAYS**

SPECIAL NOTE

In China, nutmeg (*Myristica fragrans*) is known as *rou dou kou*, and until the seventeenth century in that country it was used to cure problems of the digestive tract.

Giant Shells au Gratin

INGREDIENTS

serves 4

4/5 lb. – 350 g GIANT SHELL PASTA
SALT to taste
2 oz. HAM, in one piece
4 oz. – 150 g FONTINA CHEESE
2 EGG YOLKS
2 tablespoons – 30 g BUTTER
2 tablespoons GRATED PARMESAN

For the béchamel
1/4 CUP – 50 G BUTTER
2 tablespoons – 50 g WHITE FLOUR
ABOUT 1 CUP MILK
SALT and PEPPER to taste
pinch of NUTMEG

EQUIPMENT

a pot, a skillet
a bowl, a baking dish
a serving dish

Difficulty	**AVERAGE**
Preparation Time	**15 MIN.**
Cooking Time	**1 HOUR**
Method of cooking	**STOVETOP AND OVEN**
Microwave	**YES**
Freezing	**YES**
Keeping Time	**2 DAYS**

SPECIAL NOTE

Fontina is the best-known cheese from Val d'Aosta. Its name probably refers either to the fact that it melts, or to a Val d'Aosta location, in particular the Fontin Alps.

RECOMMENDED WINES
San Colombano (Lombardy): light red wine served at 57°F / 14°C
Taburno rosato (Campania): rosé served at 57°F / 14°C

1 Cook the shells in a pot with a generous amount of boiling salted water. When cooked, drain and place separately on a dishcloth. Cut the ham into cubes and the fontina into thin slices, put into a bowl and set aside. Preheat oven to 400°F.

2 Melt the butter in a skillet, add the flour and sauté. Pour in the milk, season with salt, freshly ground pepper and a pinch of nutmeg, and stirring constantly with a wooden spoon, cook the sauce for about 10 minutes.

3 A few minutes before removing the béchamel from the heat, add the fontina, which should melt, and the ham. Remove the mixture from the flame, add the egg yolks one at a time, stirring constantly, and fill the shells with the warm mixture.

4 Place the filled shells close together in a buttered baking dish, with the filling portion facing up. Melt the remaining butter and pour over them, then sprinkle with grated parmesan and brown them in the over for 20–25 minutes. Transfer to a heated serving dish and serve, garnishing with a few aromatic herbs.

PRACTICAL SUGGESTIONS
Your guests will appreciate this nutritious first course even more if you add a spoonful of truffle paste to the béchamel sauce after you've prepared it.

Leek and Bean Tortelloni

INGREDIENTS

serves 4

1/2 lb. – 200 g DRY BORLOTTI BEANS
1 BAY leaf
3 leaves SAGE
1 clove GARLIC
1 sprig ROSEMARY
1/4 lb. – 100 g SWISS CHARD
2 LEEKS, 1/8 cup – 30 g BUTTER
SALT and PEPPER to taste
1/2 lb. – 200 ROMAN RICOTTA
4 tablespoons GRATED PARMESAN CHEESE
1 EGG, 3/4 lb. – 300 g FRESH EGG PASTA
1 EGG WHITE,
3 tablespoons CREAM

EQUIPMENT

a mixing bowl, a saucepan, a vegetable mill
a small frying pan, a bowl, a toothed pastry
cutting wheel a small saucepan, a pot,
a baking dish

Difficulty	**AVERAGE**
Preparation Time	**30 MIN. + 12 HOURS**
Cooking Time	**1 HOUR 30 MIN.**
Method of cooking	**STOVETOP AND OVEN**
Microwave	**YES**
Freezing	**NO**
Keeping Time	**1 DAY**

SPECIAL NOTE

The leek (*Allium porrum*) is a herbaceous plant
from the Liliaceae family. It is biennial, but the
plant can be harvested at the end of the first
year of cultivation.

RECOMMENDED WINES
Bardolino chiaretto (Veneto): rosé served at 57°F / 14°C
Savuto rosato (Calabria): rosé served at 57°F / 14°C

1 Soak the beans in water for 12 hours. Drain, wash and place in a saucepan. Cover with water, add the bay leaf, sage, the garlic clove and the rosemary. Salt and bring to a boil. Cook for an hour over moderate heat, then drain and put through the vegetable mill, and place the purée in a mixing bowl. Clean the Swiss chard and cut into strips. Clean and mince the leeks, sauté in the butter in a small frying pan along with the chard for 8–10 minutes and season with salt and pepper. Add four tablespoons of bean purée and dry over moderate heat, then remove from the heat and cool. Mash the ricotta in a mixing bowl with a wooden spoon, add a tablespoon of parmesan, the leek and bean mixture, the egg, and salt and pepper.

2 Roll the pasta and cut strips about 4 inches – 10 centimeters wide. Brush the edges with egg white. Place numerous little heaps of the filling at regular distances in the center of each half strip, fold it over, press with your fingers to be sure the pasta is sealed well, and cut out the tortelloni with a toothed pastry wheel. Place the remaining bean puree in a small saucepan, add the cream, salt and pepper and bring to a boil, stirring, until you obtain a dense cream. Boil a generous amount of water in a pot, salt it and cook the tortelloni. Remove when al dente, season with the prepared sauce, place in a baking dish and sprinkle with the remaining parmesan. Bake at 400°F until browned. Serve hot.

PRACTICAL SUGGESTIONS

If you want to make a lighter sauce for these hearty tortelloni, you can use melted butter and sage instead of the bean sauce, or any leftover sauce from a roast.

Ravioli with Meat

INGREDIENTS

serves 4

For the pasta

2 full cups — 250 g WHITE FLOUR

2 EGGS, SALT to taste

For the filling

6 oz. — 150 g BONELESS BEEF

1 ONION, 1 oz. — 20 g BUTTER

4 tablespoons — 50 g FAT (lard or shortening)

SALT and PEPPER to taste

1 teaspoon minced MARJORAM

NUTMEG to taste

CINNAMON to taste, 1 EGG

For the Seasoning

1/4 cup — 50 g BUTTER

EQUIPMENT

a rolling pin, a small saucepan,
a mixing bowl a round pasta cutter about
1.5 inches — 4 cm in diameter
a pot, a frying pan

Difficulty	**AVERAGE**
Preparation Time	**40 MIN. + 30 MIN.**
Cooking Time	**30 MIN.**
Method of cooking	**STOVETOP**
Microwave	**NO**
Freezing	**YES**
Keeping Time	**3 DAYS**

SPECIAL NOTE

Cinnamon *(Cinnamomum zeylanicum)* is obtained
from the bark of cinnamon tree seedlings (a
native of Sri Lanka), which are cut at the base
every two years, during the rainy season.

1 Mound the flour and break an egg into the center. Add a pinch of salt and work the dough for about 10 minutes, until it becomes smooth and firm. Roll it out into a thin sheet and then let it rest for a half hour in a cool place.

2 Mince the meat and the onion, then place in a small saucepan to sauté with the butter for about 20 minutes, turning frequently. Place the sautéed meat and onion in a mixing bowl, add the minced kidney fat, a pinch of salt and freshly ground pepper, and season with the marjoram, nutmeg and cinnamon. Mix everything together and then add the egg to bind the ingredients.

3 Take the sheet of pasta and cut out numerous disks about 1.5 inches — 4 centimeters in diameter. Place a little heap of filling on each one, cover with another disk and press firmly on the edges to seal.

4 In a pot, bring a generous amount of salted water to boil, throw in the ravioli, mix and cook for several minutes, then drain. Melt the butter in a large frying pan, add the ravioli and sauté for 2 minutes, then serve hot.

PRACTICAL SUGGESTIONS

To shorten preparation time, you can prepare the filling the day before and store it in the refrigerator. If you have any leftover pot roast, you can use it instead of the beef, and use 2 oz. — 50 g bacon instead of the kidney fat.

Ravioli with Mushroom Sauce

INGREDIENTS
serves 4

2 oz. – 50 g DRIED PORCINI MUSHROOMS
2.5 oz. – 70 g WALNUT KERNELS
1 handful BREAD CRUMBS
1 1/2 cloves GARLIC
1/4 cup MILK or CREAM
3 tablespoons EXTRA VIRGIN OLIVE OIL
1 sprig PARSLEY
VEGETABLE BROTH as necessary
1 1/2 lb. – 600 g FRESH RAVIOLI
SALT to taste
2 handfuls GRATED PARMESAN

EQUIPMENT
a bowl
a blender
a frying pan
a pot

Difficulty	**AVERAGE**
Preparation Time	**20 MIN.**
Cooking Time	**40 MIN.**
Method of cooking	**STOVETOP**
Microwave	**NO**
Freezing	**NO**
Keeping Time	**2 DAYS**

SPECIAL NOTE
Garlic *(Allium sativum)* is one of the oldest and most venerated of cultivated plants. It grows wild in central Asia, but it is believed that its natural habitat is the Mediterranean.

RECOMMENDED WINES
Barbera del Monferrato (Piedmont): light red wine served at 61°F / 16°C
Colli Piacentini Bonarda (Emilia–Romagna): light red wine served at 61°F / 16°C

1 Soften the dried mushrooms in a bowl of lukewarm water for about a half hour. Place the walnut kernels, the breadcrumbs, a half a clove of peeled garlic, and the milk or cream, in the blender, and blend until it becomes a smooth, uniform sauce. Set aside.

2 Squeeze the mushrooms and sauté in a frying pan with the oil and remaining peeled clove of garlic, boil down all the liquid they produce, then salt them, moisten them with a small ladle of broth, cook for about 20 minutes, adding a bit of broth, and at the end add the washed and finely minced parsley.

3 In the meantime, bring a generous amount of water to boil in a pot, salt it and cook the ravioli al dente. When they are ready, drain, turn them into the frying pan with the mushroom sauce, and sauté for about a minute. Season with the prepared walnut sauce and sprinkle generously with grated parmesan, mix well to blend the ingredients, and serve immediately

PRACTICAL SUGGESTIONS
This sauce can be used to season both meat ravioli and cheese ravioli. You can use 4/5 lb.– 350 g fresh porcini mushrooms in place of the dried ones; clean them well with a damp cloth and slice. Then proceed as indicated.

108

Ricotta Ravioli with Saffron

INGREDIENTS
serves 4

For the pasta
3 1/2 cups – 400 g WHITE FLOUR
4 EGGS

For the filling
1 pinch SAFFRON
1 tablespoon MILK
4/5 lb. – 350 g RICOTTA
the grated peel of ONE ORANGE
NUTMEG to taste
1 EGG
SALT to taste

For the sauce
GRATED PARMESAN to taste
1/4 cup – 50 g BUTTER
1 sprig ROSEMARY

EQUIPMENT
1 small bowl, a mixing bowl, a pot
a slotted spoon

Difficulty	AVERAGE
Preparation Time	30 MIN. + 40 MIN.
Cooking Time	15 MIN.
Method of cooking	STOVETOP
Microwave	NO
Freezing	YES
Keeping Time	2 DAYS

SPECIAL NOTE
Saffron consists of dried stamens of the crocus (*Crocus sativus*), which originates in Asia Minor. To produce 1 lb. of saffron, you need 100,000 flowers.

RECOMMENDED WINES
Franciacorta white (Lombardy): dry white wine served at 50°F / 10°C
Verdicchio di Matelica (Marche): mellow, aromatic white wine served at 50°F / 10°C

1 Mound the flour on a cutting board, break the eggs in the middle, beat them lightly with a fork, and work the dough with your hands until it becomes smooth. Let it rest for at least 20 minutes, wrapped in a clean dishcloth, then roll it out.

2 Dissolve the saffron in a small bowl with the milk. In a mixing bowl, mix the ricotta with a wooden spoon for a few minutes, and add the saffron, orange peel, a bit of powdered nutmeg, the egg and a pinch of salt, and mix one more time to blend everything well.

3 Spread this mixture on half the rolled–out pasta, in spoonfuls placed at a regular distance from each other, then fold the other half of the pasta over it and cut out the ravioli. Let them rest for about 15 minutes on a dishcloth sprinkled with a bit of flour.

4 Bring a generous amount of salted water to boil in a large pot, add the ravioli, and as soon as they float to the top, push them back down with a slotted spoon, continuing until they are all cooked al dente. Drain, sprinkle with grated parmesan and season with the butter browned with the rosemary. Serve.

PRACTICAL SUGGESTIONS
To make this recipe lower in calories and at the same time obtain a one-dish meal, season the ravioli with vegetables chopped into matchstick slices and sauté in a bit of olive oil.

Baked Green Ravioli

INGREDIENTS

serves 4

1 1/2 lb. – 600 g GREEN RAVIOLI
WITH CHEESE
scarce 1/4 cup – 40 g MELTED BUTTER
4 EGG YOLKS
4 tablespoons CREAM
SALT and PEPPER to taste
pinch of NUTMEG
3 EGG WHITES
4 oz. – 100 g HAM in one piece
4 heaping tablespoons GRATED PARMESAN
4 oz. – 100 g WALNUT KERNELS

EQUIPMENT

a pot
a mixing bowl
a bowl
an oval baking dish

Difficulty	**EASY**
Preparation Time	**15 MIN.**
Cooking Time	**35 MIN.**
Method of cooking	**STOVETOP AND OVEN**
Microwave	**YES**
Freezing	**YES**
Keeping Time	**2 DAYS**

SPECIAL NOTE

Egg white contains emulsifying substances
(lecithin) that incorporate little air bubbles as it
is beaten. This is what makes it expand as it is
whipped.

RECOMMENDED WINES
Chianti classico (Tuscany): medium–bodied red wine served at 61°F / 16°C
Franciacorta red (Lombardy): light red wine served at 61°F / 16°C

1 Cook the ravioli in a pot with a generous amount of boiling water, drain when very al dente, place in a mixing bowl and season with the melted butter.

2 Beat the egg yolks in a bowl with the cream, a pinch of salt, freshly ground pepper and nutmeg, then blend everything with the ravioli. Mix thoroughly and then blend in the egg whites, beaten to stiff peaks.

3 Butter an oval baking dish, make a layer of ravioli, then place some of the ham on top, cut in cubes, then sprinkle with a bit of grated parmesan and coarsely chopped walnuts. Make another layer of ravioli and continue until you have finished the ingredients, being sure to finish with the ravioli.

4 Bake at 350°F until the surface becomes golden brown. Serve immediately in the baking dish.

PRACTICAL SUGGESTIONS

The egg whites will whip into peaks faster if you add a pinch of fine salt or a bit of lemon juice. To prevent them from sticking to the container in which they are being whipped, run it under cold water first. If you have any leftover ravioli, you can reuse them the next day, seasoning them with a bit of melted butter and reheating them in the oven.

Tortellini Royale

RECOMMENDED WINES

Grignolino d'Asti (Piedmont): light red wine served at 61°F / 16°C
Rossese di Dolceacqua (Liguria): light red wine served at 61°F / 16°C

1 Mix the ricotta in a bowl for a minute with a wooden spoon, add the cream and blend well. Mixing gently, blend in the parmesan, sprinkle in a generous amount of nutmeg, and season with salt and freshly ground pepper. Slice the prosciutto, heat it in a frying pan with the butter, add it to the cream and ricotta mixture, and keep warm.

2 Preheat the oven to 350°F. Bring a generous amount of water to boil in a pot, salt it and throw in the tortellini. Cook al dente, drain well and transfer to a buttered baking dish.

3 Cover the tortellini with the prepared sauce, sprinkle with minced parsley and mix, blending the ingredients well. Bake in the oven for 4–5 minutes, or until the surface is browned. Remove from the oven and serve in the baking dish.

INGREDIENTS
serves 4

1/2 lb.– 200 g RICOTTA
5 tablespoons – 50 g CREAM
3 tablespoons – 50 g GRATED PARMESAN
NUTMEG to taste
SALT and PEPPER to taste
2 oz.– 50 g PROSCIUTTO
a walnut-sized chunk of BUTTER
18 oz. – 500 g TORTELLINI
1 tablespoon minced PARSLEY

EQUIPMENT
a mixing bowl
a pot
a baking dish

Difficulty	**AVERAGE**
Preparation Time	**10 MIN.**
Cooking Time	**20 MIN.**
Method of cooking	**STOVETOP AND OVEN**
Microwave	**NO**
Freezing	**YES**
Keeping Time	**2 DAYS**

PRACTICAL SUGGESTIONS
If you use dry tortellini for this recipe, you can prevent them from breaking during cooking by immersing them in cold water for a few minutes, then removing them and tossing them in a pot of lukewarm water, which is then brought to a boil. Then, transfer them to another pot of salted boiling water, and cook until done.

SPECIAL NOTE
According to one version of the *Secchia Rapita*, tortellini take their form from a "squint-eyed Bolognese" innkeeper, who was inspired by the navel of the sleeping goddess Venus.

Ravioli della Val Pusteria

INGREDIENTS

serves 4

For the filling

1 1/2 lb. – 600 g SPINACH
pinch of POWDERED CUMIN
pinch of SALT

For the pasta

1 lb. – 400 g RYE FLOUR
SALT to taste
a walnut-sized chunk of BUTTER
1 EGG
MILK as necessary

For cooking

OLIVE OIL for frying

EQUIPMENT

a pot, a frying pan
a slotted spoon
absorbent paper towels

Difficulty	**AVERAGE**
Preparation Time	**30 MIN.**
Cooking Time	**40 MIN.**
Method of cooking	**STOVETOP**
Microwave	**NO**
Freezing	**NO**
Keeping Time	**2 DAYS**

SPECIAL NOTE

Spinach was once known as "vegetable blood" due to its proverbially high iron content. It also contains large quantities of vitamins A and C.

RECOMMENDED WINES
Trentino bianco (Trentino): dry white wine served at 50°F / 10°C
Bolgheri rosato (Tuscany): rosé served at 57°F / 14°C

1 Trim the spinach, wash repeatedly under running water and cook 15 minutes in a pot with a small amount of salted water. Drain, squeeze, and mince, mixing in the cumin.

2 Mound the flour on the cutting board, add a pinch of salt, the butter softened to room temperature, and the egg to the middle, and mix together, gradually adding enough milk to make a dough of the right consistency. Roll it out thinly and cut into squares 1 1/2–2 inches (4–5 centimeters) long

3 Place a bit of the filling in the middle of each square, cover with another square and seal the edges well by pressing with your fingertips.

4 Heat a generous amount of oil in a frying pan or fryer, and when it is hot, add the ravioli. Let them brown on all sides, then remove with a slotted spoon and place on absorbent paper towels to remove any excess grease, and serve hot.

PRACTICAL SUGGESTIONS
Spinach has many uses, outside the kitchen as well. For example, you can reuse spinach cooking water to clean black wool garments. A good remedy for burns is to apply spinach leaves cooked in olive oil.

Duck Tortellini with Vegetable Sauce

INGREDIENTS

serves *4*

For the pasta

6 tablespoons — 150 g WHITE FLOUR

4 tablespoons — 100 g SUPERFINE/CAKE FLOUR

2 EGGS, 1 EGG WHITE, a pinch of SALT

For the filling

1/2 ONION, 2/3 lb. — 250 g DUCK BREAST

spoons RED WINE, 3/4 lb. — 300 g SPINACH,

1 EGG, 1 SPRIG THYME, 2 oz. — 1 handful leaves

PARSLEY, SALT and PEPPER to taste

2 tablespoons EXTRA VIRGIN OLIVE OIL, 5 table

For the sauce

1 EGGPLANT, 1 CARROT, 2 ZUCCHINI

1/2 lb. — 200 g STRING BEANS

2 oz. — 1 bunch BASIL, 1/3 cup — 70 g BUTTER

SALT and PEPPER to taste

6 oz. — 150 g SHELLED PEAS

EQUIPMENT

2 saucepans, a frying pan, a bowl

a pastry wheel with teeth, a pot

Difficulty	**ELABORATE**
Preparation Time	**30 MIN. + 30 MIN.**
Cooking Time	**40 MIN.**
Method of cooking	**STOVETOP**
Microwave	**YES**
Freezing	**YES**
Keeping Time	**2 DAYS**

SPECIAL NOTE

In Italy, flours are classified according to the following categories, depending on moisture content, ash, cellulose and dry gluten: type 00 flour; type 0 flour; type 1 flour; type 2 flour, and whole wheat flour.

RECOMMENDED WINES

Fara (Piedmont): light red wine served at 64°F / 18°C

Montalcino rosso (Tuscany): light red wine served at 64°F / 18°C

1 Sift the flours together. Mound them, break the eggs into the center and add the salt. Work the mixture until you obtain an elastic, uniform dough, then let it rest a half hour, wrapped in a cloth. Mince the onion and wilt it with the oil. Cut the duck breast into cubes and add it to the onion. Brown on all sides, bathing with the wine and allowing it to evaporate at high heat. Cool. Wash the spinach and sauté for a minute in a frying pan. Finely mince the cubes of meat, the thyme and the parsley; place them in a bowl and add the egg, salt and pepper. Mix with a wooden spoon until the ingredients are blended.

2 Roll the pasta very thinly and cut into 1 1/4 – 1 1/2 inch (3–4 cm) squares. Brush the edges with lightly beaten egg white. Place a bit of filling in the center of a square, cover it with another square, and press the edges with your fingers to seal. Clean the eggplants, carrot, zucchini and string beans. Wash and cut them into cubes or strips. Wash the basil, dry and chop it. Melt the butter and add the carrot, the string beans, a quarter cup of water, salt and pepper. After 5 minutes, add the peas, and cook for another 5 minutes. Then add the zucchini and eggplant, and continue cooking for 5–6 minutes more, then sprinkle with basil. Bring a generous amount of salted water to boil, cook the ravioli, drain when al dente and season with the vegetable sauce. Serve hot.

PRACTICAL SUGGESTIONS

As only duck breast is used for these tortellini, take the meat from the remaining parts and prepare dumplings that can be served with cooked vegetables such as peas.

Agnolotti with Cardoon Cream

INGREDIENTS

serves 4

2.2 lb. – 1 kg CARDOONS
juice of one LEMON
1 SHALLOT
1 oz. – 20 g BUTTER
SALT and PEPPER to taste
3 tablespoons EXTRA VIRGIN OLIVE
1/2 cup MILK
1/2 lb. – 200 g FONTINA CHEESE
18 oz. – 500 g AGNOLOTTI
(a small, half–moon shaped pasta)
GRATED PARMESAN to taste

EQUIPMENT

a pot
a vegetable mill
a frying pan
a mixing bowl, a small saucepan
a serving dish

Difficulty	AVERAGE
Preparation Time	20 MIN.
Cooking Time	1 HOUR
Method of cooking	STOVETOP
Microwave	NO
Freezing	NO
Keeping Time	1 DAY

SPECIAL NOTE

The cardoon (*Cynara cardunculus*) is a Medeiterranean vegetable related to the artichoke, which may be substituted in its place.

Recommended Wines
Dolcetto di Dogliani (Piedmont): light red wine served at 61°F / 16°C
Valpolicella (Veneto): light red wine served at 61°F / 16°C

1 After trimming the cardoons, use the most tender stalks, cut them into small pieces, wash with lemon water to prevent them from turning brown, then cook them in a pot of salted water for 30 minutes. Drain well and put through the vegetable mill, then place the mixture in a bowl.

2 Sauté the washed, minced shallot, butter, a pinch of salt, and freshly ground pepper in a frying pan with the oil. After a few minutes, add the cardoon purée, mix well and season for 10 minutes. Then add the milk, which you have heated to lukewarm in a small saucepan, and the fontina cheese, cut into cubes. Continue to mix with a wooden spoon until the mixture becomes creamy.

3 Place a generous amount of water in a pot, and when it comes to a boil, salt it and add the agnolotti, cooking them al dente. Drain well and place in the frying pan with the cardoon cream, add the grated parmesan and mix well. Sauté the agnolotti for a few minutes, then transfer them to a heated serving dish and serve immediately.

Practical Suggestions
If you only need a few drops of lemon juice, make a little hole in the fruit and then seal it with a toothpick. If you do not have a juicer and you need all the juice, you can easily extract it by cutting the lemon in half and rotating a fork in the pulp.

Pansôti with Preboggion

INGREDIENTS

serves 4

For the pasta

3 cups — 350 g WHITE FLOUR
1/4 cup DRY WHITE WINE
SALT to taste

For the filling

1 1/2 lb. — 700 g PREBOGGION (with at least
2/3 lb. — 300 g borage)
1 clove GARLIC
6 oz. — 130 g RICOTTA,
2 heaping tablespoons GRATED PARMESAN
2 EGGS,
SALT to taste

For the seasoning

1 CUP WALNUT SAUCE

EQUIPMENT

2 pots, a vegetable mill, a mixing bowl
a slotted spatula

Difficulty	**AVERAGE**
Preparation Time	**30 MIN.**
Cooking Time	**20 MIN.**
Method of cooking	**STOVETOP**
Microwave	**NO**
Freezing	**NO**
Keeping Time	**3 DAYS**

SPECIAL NOTE

Borage flowers can be eaten raw in salad or
cooked in soups, even mixed with other herbs.
They can also be used to flavor wine and grappa.

RECOMMENDED WINES
Breganze Vespaiolo: dry white wine served at 54°F / 12°C
Alto Adige Lagrein (Alto Adige): rosé served at 57°F / 14°C

1 Prepare the pasta: mound the flour on the cutting board and pour the wine, a cup of water and a pinch of salt in the center. Work the dough for a few minutes until it becomes smooth and firm. Then roll it out thinly and cut out triangles about 2 1/2 – 3 inches (7 centimeters) long.

2 Prepare the filling: carefully trim all the vegetables, then wash and boil them in only the water leftover after washing, for about 15 minutes. When done, drain, squeeze well and put through the vegetable mill. Place the mixture in a mixing bowl. The add the peeled and minced garlic, the ricotta, the parmesan, the eggs and the salt, and mix well. Place a bit of the filling on each triangle, then fold them over, pressing firmly on the edges.

3 Heat a generous amount of salted water in a pot. When it begins to boil, add the pansôti and cook for 5–6 minutes. Then drain them gently by lifting them out with a slotted spatula, season with the walnut sauce and serve hot.

PRACTICAL SUGGESTIONS
Preboggion, used to fill pansôti (or "potbellies"), which are typical of Ligurian cuisine, is a mixture of wild edible herbs such as borage, spring cabbage, sow thistle, dog's-tooth and wild chard. However, an assortment of store-bought herbs also works well. The walnut sauce is prepared with softened bread, walnut kernels, garlic, curdled milk and oil.

Raviolini Cooked in Sauce

INGREDIENTS

serves 4

1/4 cup — 40 g BUTTER
1 ONION
1 lb. — 450 g PLUM TOMATOES
3 cups — 3/4 liter VEGETABLE BROTH
SALT and PEPPER to taste
18 oz. — 500 g FRESH SMALL RAVIOLI
a few leaves BASIL
4 tablespoons GRATED PARMESAN

EQUIPMENT

a skillet
a vegetable mill
a serving dish

Difficulty	**AVERAGE**
Preparation Time	**10 MIN.**
Cooking Time	**30 MIN.**
Method of cooking	**STOVETOP**
Microwave	**YES**
Freezing	**YES**
Keeping Time	**2 DAYS**

SPECIAL NOTE

Until the end of the 18th century, the tomato was considered an insignificant or even poisonous fruit, but later became an essential element in cooking, especially Mediterranean cuisine.

RECOMMENDED WINES
Frascati Superiore (Lazio): dry white wine served at 54°F / 12°C
Gioia del Colle bianco (Puglia): dry white wine served at 54°F / 12°C

1 Sauté half the butter with the peeled, finely minced onion in a skillet. When it begins to turn golden brown, add the tomatoes, which you have put through the vegetable mill, and their juices. Let it season for a few minutes, then add the boiling broth and a pinch of salt and freshly ground pepper.

2 Bring to a boil, add the ravioli and the washed, dried basil, cover the skillet, leaving it open a crack, and continue cooking for about 20 minutes. Mix from time to time with a wooden spoon.

3 Add hot broth if the sauce becomes too thick, or else reduce it over high heat for the last few minutes of cooking if it is too thin. Transfer to a serving dish and serve the ravioli after blending in the remaining butter and grated parmesan.

PRACTICAL SUGGESTIONS
If you follow the above cooking directions, you will not have to use a colander. If you like, the sauce can be enriched with the addition of minced mushrooms, carrots and celery.